Other Telecom Titles from Aegis Publishing Group:

Telecom Business Opportunities
The Entrepreneur's Guide to Making Money in the Telecommunications Revolution, by Steven Rosenbush
$24.95   1-890154-04-0

Getting the Most From Your Yellow Pages Advertising
by Barry Maher
$19.95   1-890154-05-9

Telecom Glossary
Understanding Telecommunications Technology, by Marc Robins
$9.95   1-890154-02-4

Telecom Made Easy
Money-Saving, Profit-Building Solutions for Home Businesses, Telecommuters and Small Organizations, by June Langhoff
$19.95   0-9632790-7-6

The Telecommuter's Advisor
Working in the Fast Lane, by June Langhoff
$14.95   0-9632790-5-X

900 Know-How
How to Succeed With Your Own 900 Number Business,
by Robert Mastin
$19.95   0-9632790-3-3

The Business Traveler's Survival Guide
How to Get Work Done While on the Road, by June Langhoff
$9.95   1-890154-03-2

Phone Company Services
Working Smarter With the Right Telecom Tools, by June Langhoff
$9.95   1-890154-01-6

Money-Making 900 Numbers
How Entrepreneurs Use the Telephone to Sell Information
by Carol Morse Ginsburg and Robert Mastin
$19.95   0-9632790-1-7

Winning Communications Strategies

*How Small Businesses Master
Cutting-Edge Technology
to Stay Competitive, Provide Better
Service and Make More Money*

Written by:
Jeffrey Kagan

Aegis Publishing Group, Ltd.
796 Aquidneck Avenue
Newport, Rhode Island 02842
401-849-4200
www.aegisbooks.com

Library of Congress Catalog Card Number: 97-72690

International Standard Book Number: 0-9632790-8-4

Printed in the United States of America.

10 9 8 7 6 5 4 3 2 1

This publication is designed to provide accurate and authoritative information in regard to the subject matter covered. It is sold with the understanding that neither the author nor the publisher are engaged in rendering legal, accounting or other professional service. If legal advice or other expert assistance is required, the services of a competent professional should be sought.

Publisher's Cataloging In Publication Data
Kagan, Jeffrey
Winning Communications Strategies: How Small Businesses Master Cutting-Edge Technology to Stay Competitive, Provide Better Service and Make More Money / by Jeffrey Kagan.

1. Telecommunications.
TK5101.L35   1997   621.382   97-72690
ISBN 0-9632790-8-4

Acknowledgements

Writing a book is always a time-consuming and intense process, even when it's a labor of love. But in the final weeks, when the intensity is white hot, it's the support of your family and friends that makes the difference.

Thanks to my kids, Jason, Adam and Jennifer, for dealing with an absentee, sometimes grumpy dad while I holed myself in my home office to plug away for countless hours. Thanks to my bride, best friend and most senior and trusted advisor, Deborah, for being my biggest fan and reality-checker all rolled into one.

Thanks to my editor Francis "Nim" Marsh who helped keep the manuscript flowing by correcting all the flaws I couldn't see by being too close to the forest to see the trees. Thanks to my publisher, Bob Mastin, who had faith that I'd get done on time, which I almost pulled off.

Contents

Introduction

A Nation in Transition
Creates New Opportunities

This book is about making money and doing business in the '90s and beyond. It's about integrating the new telecommunications tools and information technologies in our businesses to increase sales, keep customers happy, and have fun in the process. About breaking the rules and writing new ones to gain competitive advantage.

The Telecommunications Act of 1996 changed everything. Its purpose is to tear down the artificial walls separating different parts of the telecom business. It allows local and long-distance companies—and all the other players—into each other's business, and it fuels the explosion of new services and technologies you can use to improve your business. Telecom reform threw out the old rule book, and the new rules are being rewritten as you read these words.

We are a nation in transition. 1996 was the first year that computers outsold color televisions. E-mail and faxes are impacting the postal service, and Americans are forsaking television in increasing numbers and going online, which is causing the major television networks to rethink their strategies and markets. What's going on here? Everything is changing.

Some of the more valuable lessons are learned by watching what others are doing successfully, and then duplicating it in our own businesses. By watching others use technology to address their business problems, we can jump-start our own creativity to come up with new solutions to our own challenges. All of the sudden we have a blinding flash—an *AHA!*—we'd never thought of before. That's what this book is about. If you pick up just one good idea and implement it profitably, the time invested reading this book will have been well spent.

Because I have been quoted so often in the media—and through exposure from my writing columns and giving speeches at dozens of business meetings, seminars and conferences—I have developed an increasingly high profile. Over the years, this has provided a unique opportunity to talk with, hear from, and interview hundreds of entrepreneurs and business people. The ideas and stories in this book have come from these encounters.

Some of the names in this book are real. Others have been changed, as an acquaintance once said, "to protect the stupid." But as I reminded him, there are no stupid mistakes today. Everyone is a little confused. Everyone is experimenting. Everyone is making stupid mistakes, and everyone is more tolerant of mistakes than ever before. So now is the time to be playing around with all this stuff. Customers aren't expecting you to have it right, yet.

A warning, however: That grace period won't last forever. What is a competitive advantage today will simply be a core business tool—the basic price of admission—tomorrow. In a few short years, customers will assume that you have gone through the learning curve, and they'll be expecting you to know what you are doing. Your competitors will know what *they* are doing.

So dig in now. Make mistakes now, when it's still okay to be less than perfect. The only really stupid mistake you can make is to sit this one out, thinking this information-age thing is a fad, expecting this revolution to blow by so things can return to the way they were. That's what the buggy-whip makers did when the horseless carriage was invented. And you know what happened to them.

The names may or may not be real, but the stories, strategies and lessons are. My goal with this book is to help you think about your business, your customers, and your competitors in new ways. To help you look at your challenges and come up with new solutions to old problems by watching what other successful business people are doing.

This book is intended to help you understand and leverage the opportunities created by the historic transition our nation is undergoing. To help you develop strategies for winning new customers and for keeping existing ones. To help you develop your own... **Winning Communications Strategies!**

Jeffrey Kagan
Atlanta, Georgia

Chapter 1
Big Picture Overview

Understanding the Forces and the Changes
Reshaping the Way We Conduct Business

In order to understand all the changes that are occurring and to benefit from the resulting opportunities, we first must have a framework to work within. We need to step back to get a clear, big-picture understanding of what's happening. An overview of the forces reshaping the way we do business.

Changing Customer Demands

The first thing we have to realize is that we are getting spoiled. We are accustomed to easy, instant access to information and communications. To never being out of touch. To getting what we want, when we want it. To demanding the best service and not tolerating anything less than excellence. We are increasingly busy in our own businesses as they become more complex and competitive.

Surprise! Our customers are getting spoiled, too. They expect and demand more than ever before, quicker than ever before. It's harder to satisfy customers these days, and keeping them satisfied is crucial to keeping them at all.

Don't you just love the '90s? Call it life in the fast lane, but for customers, waiting a few hours for a return phone call, or a few days for information to arrive in the mail, is no longer acceptable. They want what they want NOW. They want the highest level of quality and service. They want superior responsiveness. They want answers and information. They want flawless execution. And they want it immediately. And if you can't step up to the plate and give them what they want, in the blink of an eye they will find one of your competitors who can. And the last thing you'll hear them say will be: "It's been nice working with you; don't let the door hit you on the way out."

Business in the '90s

For better or for worse, that's the fast-paced state of today's business world. Fax machines, computers, e-mail, voice mail—all supposed to allow us to do more in less time so we can have more free time. *Ha!* Instead, we are expected to do more in less time and work all the time. What went wrong?

While discussions of the societal issues are banter for another book, let's just say that this is the hand we've been dealt. We can either complain all the way to the poor house, or use the change and chaos to our advantage and laugh all the way to the bank. The choice is that simple. And by the way, being confused into inaction is not a valid excuse. Like a deer caught in the headlights, too many small businesses are frozen in the glare of the information and communications revolution. That same fate awaits those who do not act.

It's not like there's much of a choice. There's no such thing as standing still. You are either moving ahead or falling behind. Remember what happened to the buggy-whip industry when the horseless carriage was invented? Many successful buggy-whip makers didn't believe the world was changing and continued to do things in the same old way. When was the last time you needed a buggy whip?

The Choice

The advancements in anytime/anyplace communications are driving a revolution. You have two clear choices. Either you can fight the change and chaos and insist on doing things the way you've always done them—just like the buggy whip guys—or you can look for ways to exploit the relentless and unstoppable march of change. Loads of new opportunities are created by change. Just look at the *Forbes* list of the wealthiest 400 people. For the first time the list is topped by the likes of Bill Gates and Warren Buffet, people who deal in the realm of ideas and information rather than the traditional assortment of industrialists and real estate magnates.

Longer Term Historical Perspective

The way we create wealth in this country is changing. We are encountering change on a scale akin to that of a century ago. Back then, the telephone and the automobile were invented, which changed the way we communicated, shared and distributed information and news, moved product and services, and conducted business. Those inventions changed our economy and our society, and they changed the rules.

We are going through the same kind of change today, but the revolution is being powered by the computer chip and the communications networks. Insofar as anything is possible in the digital world, we are going to see more change in the next decade than we've seen in our entire lifetimes. This will be an incredible time full of new opportunities. If you've envied the Rockefellers, Carnegies and Fords for the era in which they thrived, envy no more. The opportunity created by this digital age is unrivaled. Just look at all the 20-something software multimillionaires. *Yahooooooooooo!*

You don't have to strike out in new directions to be successful. You just have to utilize all the new technologies to revolutionize your business, and, by doing so, do things better than your competition.

Competitive Advantage

Companies that embrace all the new communications services and technologies and integrate them into their businesses have a significant competitive advantage. Such a policy enables them to protect their customers from new competitors and, at the same time, allows them to move into new markets.

Beware: The same factors that allow you to enter and exploit new markets and new opportunities, with fewer barriers to entry, also allow your competitors, new and old, to move into *your* business. Your customers are at risk. Think about it. Whether you started your business two or 20 years ago, you were forced to use the technology of the day. If you were to start your business today, it would look, act and work very differently. This is the advantage your new competitors have over your entrenched operation. The same advantage you could have in other markets.

As competitors embrace new communications and information technology, they can often provide a better quality of service, more efficiently and at a lower cost. This raises the bar of customer expectations and demands. Your customers will quickly learn of the advantages of doing business with your competitors. If you are darned lucky, they may give you the chance to get up-to-speed. Chances are, however, that they will just start using the other guys without so much as a *Dear John* letter.

Not If, But When

It's not a question of *if* you'll embrace these new technologies and integrate them into your business. It's only a question of *when*. More to the point, it's a question of whether you'll recognize the forces that are reshaping the way we do business and seize the new opportunities *in time*.

For example, maybe you think you will never need to use video conferencing, but what if both your competitors and your customers are using it? And they prefer to use it. You are at risk of losing them if you don't join them. It's not a question of *if*; it's only a question of *when*.

This book is not intended to be a textbook of all of today's technologies. Rather, it's purpose is to illustrate how other small businesses are leveraging new communications technologies in their companies to do more business, make money, save money, improve customer service, increase sales—and stay competitive.

Chapter 2
Who Ya Gonna Call?

Turn to Your Phone Companies for Answers

How do you get "up to speed" and "keep up" with all the latest communications services and technology? After all, you've got a business to run. The average entrepreneur wants to take advantage of all the new technology, but has neither the time nor interest in becoming a telecommunications expert.

In the past, large businesses spent fortunes on armies of consultants and technical experts to wade through the competing choices and conflicting claims. Small businesses didn't have that luxury. They typically had to fend for themselves with, at best, a piecemeal approach. But that's no longer the case. In fact, one of your best resources is working for you already—your phone company. That's right, believe it or not. The folks who provide you with local or long-distance telephone services, equipment, cellular, paging, Internet access, e-mail, and so on, have armies of highly-trained experts just waiting for your call.

Changing Role of the Phone Company

Thanks to the Telecommunications Act of 1996, the rules and roles are changing. The role of the telephone company is changing. And the role of the telephone company sales and customer-service representative is changing. There is no such thing as a plain-old phone company anymore. They are evolving into full-service providers of all the communications and information services you need.

The goal is to offer a complete selection of local, long-distance, e-mail, voice mail, Internet access and hosting, cellular, paging, PCS, data, news and information, entertainment, electronic commerce and more. Bundling of everything you need under one roof. One-stop shops. And they are making great progress. Today, you can now get most of these services from one place, albeit not as seamlessly as you will be able to in the next few years. But just like it's okay for you to make mistakes, it's okay for them to do the same. For awhile, anyway.

The point is that there is no way to have a massive change in an industry and a massive transformation of its players without a few bumps in the road. What is important is that the nation's phone companies are rapidly evolving into resource centers that can help small businesses improve efficiency and compete successfully.

Changing Focus: From Sales toward Consultants and Advisors

Sales and service reps are becoming consultants, advisors and teachers—more interested in developing a longer-term, multi-faceted relationship, than scoring a quick slam-dunk sale to meet quota. They no longer focus solely on bringing in business, but also growing the business they already have. They are moving away from being hunters to being farmers, cultivating and growing relationships with customers.

Moving away from an acquisition strategy toward a retention strategy is a fundamental shift in thinking for the phone companies. Don't get me wrong. You'll still get plenty of sales calls both in the office and at the dinner table. They are still very interested in acquiring new business. However, they never paid much attention to retaining customers before. All the focus was on bringing in new business with little emphasis placed on keeping customers.

That's changing, and it's a valuable change for the small-business customer, because the phone companies want to make you happy. They want to keep you around and win even more of your business as they continue to expand their service offerings.

New Focus on Small-Business Market

In the past, phone companies never paid much attention to the small-business market. Larger businesses and consumers at both ends of the spectrum got the lion's share of care and focus. Small businesses again were left to fend for themselves—until recently.

All of a sudden, in the last few years, the booming small-business market has popped up in a big way on the radar screens at the nation's phone companies. They have set up small-business units or special programs. They have introduced a wide array of services and resources targeted and tailored specifically to the needs of small businesses.

Some even have hybrid services that allow a SOHO (Small Office/Home Office) customer to blend home and office calling into one combined service. Let's face it, that's how many of us work. The lines between home and office—work and play—are blurring. We are doing more work from home than ever before. More than 40 million Americans work either full-time or part-time from home, which has led to the proliferation of communications products and services for this growing market.

Staying on the Cutting Edge of Technology

Continuously upgrading systems and equipment is a very expensive and time-intensive process. Yet, if keeping on the cutting edge is vital to success, how is a small business to keep up?

Once again, the phone companies are the logical ally. They continue to install and upgrade to the newest technology. They have to; it's their business. Smart business people are recognizing the power of using the phone company's products and services as a way of staying on the cutting edge. Let the big guys spend fortunes installing, maintaining and upgrading their systems. Small businesses don't have time. They have a business to run.

The phone companies spend billions every year keeping their systems state-of-the-art, so you don't have to. They not only improve and upgrade what they have, but they continuously bring out new products and services to address new and ongoing needs of small businesses. Having regular meetings with your telephone company reps can enlighten you to new ways of serving your customers better. This saves you lots of time by having new solutions come to you, rather than you having to seek them out on your own. If you can find the time in the first place.

Look at your phone company as an advisor in telecommunications and technology. If you don't trust your phone company, it's time to find one you do. A phone company should not be an adversary, but, rather, a part of your advisory council. Its representatives talk with loads of small businesses, and they can often recommend solutions you wouldn't think of on your own. Plus, they have whole departments of people who lie awake nights just thinking how they can serve you and keep you happy so you won't be lost to the competition. That's a pretty powerful position for most small businesses to be in.

Untangling the Web

All phone companies have a presence on the Internet. Go to their World Wide Web (WWW) sites and you'll find a wealth of information for small businesses—from case histories, products and services to educational materials for running a small business. You'll also find loads of links to other small business and telecommunications resources. It's amazing how much information is actually available for free on the Web. Finding plenty of information isn't a problem anymore. However, sorting through it all and becoming an information archeologist is a challenge.

Here is a list of some of the top phone company World Wide Web sites, in alphabetical order:

Ameritech	www.ameritech.com
AT&T	www.att.com
Bell Atlantic	www.bell-atl.com
Bell Canada	www.bell.ca
BellSouth	www.bellsouth.com
Frontier	www.frontiercorp.com
GTE	www.gte.com
LCI	www.lci.com
LDDS/Worldcom	www.wcom.com
MCI	www.mci.com
Nynex	www.nynex.com
Pacific Tel	www.pactel.com
SBC	www.sbc.com
SNET	www.snet.com
Sprint	www.sprint.com
US WEST	www.uswest.com

Other Sources

In addition to your various phone companies, there are other sources of products, services and answers. The big office supply stores like Office Depot, Office Max and Staples sell a wide variety of telecom products for the home and office. Electronics stores such as Radio Shack and Circuit City, and mail order firms like Hello Direct (800-444-3556), are also great sources. Don't overlook telephone and computer equipment vendors and resellers in your area. They are often a great source of advice and products. For more sophisticated telephone services, try a telecommunications service bureau, usually listed in the Yellow Pages under *Telecommunications Services*.

Best Place to Start

So, for a small business, one of the first places to turn for guidance through the maze and confusion of the information and communications revolution is, without a doubt, your phone company, and various communications service providers in your area. These companies may keep us confused with a barrage of conflicting claims and confusing choices in their advertisements, but when we talk to their representatives one-to-one, it's a different story.

Your phone company is spending a fortune training its people to be there for you. It is continuously upgrading its technology and systems, and rolling out new offerings to help you find solutions to your business problems. It's a valuable resource that you can't afford to ignore, and it's the most logical starting place for any small business.

Chapter 3
Wireless Strategies

No More Missed Opportunities

Chicago was hit by a massive ice storm (so what's new?) and Mike Nikolich found himself out in the cold. As the president of Tech Image, Ltd., a Palatine, Ill., public relations firm, his office was without power or phones for 48 hours. Just after the lights went out, an editor in New Jersey, who needed a story Tech Image had written, finally reached Nikolich by pager. He promptly called the editor back using his cellphone. All he had to do was get the story to the editor within the hour and he'd be a hero to his client. Piece of cake right? Remember no phones and no power. Oh well, there's always overnight delivery. . .

Unfortunately, the East Coast was experiencing even worse weather. "Because road conditions were so bad in New Jersey, traditional overnight delivery services wouldn't guarantee delivery for one week, so that obviously wasn't an option," says Nikolich. "In a panic, I called a friend on my cellular phone and asked if he had a cellular modem. He did. I hooked up my laptop to his car phone and completed transmission of the story to the editor just as the power drained from my PC with one last telling *beeeeeep*. We made our deadline and received a cover story to boot!"

The Telecommunications Act of 1996 threw gasoline on an already explosive telecom industry. I get called by reporters every day for comments on telecom news items. I enjoy the constant flow of ideas and questions. It keeps me on my toes. However, Wednesday, May 8, 1997 was even busier than usual. The FCC announced plans for revising key provisions in the process of telecom reform. When these events happen the floodgates open and reporters call in a continuous stream for hours. It's a challenge to keep up with the flow, but being widely quoted in this industry is an honor that I don't take lightly.

The only problem was, this day I had to get to the bank to make a transaction by 2 p.m. At 1:45, I finished an interview with *USA Today*, and knowing I might be missing opportunities to talk with other reporters, flew out the door to make the deadline with my banker. While at the bank my pager went off. It was a producer from National Public Radio wanting to do an interview on "access fee reform" for an upcoming newscast. He was on deadline and couldn't wait until I got back to the office. So from the comfort of the couch in the corner of the bank lobby, I gave a 20-minute interview over my cellphone to NPR while the banking transaction was being conducted. I made the deadline and the next morning the interview was played nationally on the morning news (of course, I missed it since I was up late the night before doing revisions for this book).

Only a few short years ago, these would have been a missed opportunities. However, Nikolich and I were able to take advantage of these opportunities thanks to the new communications tools at our disposal. But it's not good enough just to have the tools at your disposal. We have to start thinking in new ways. Thinking creatively. There's nothing we can't do when it comes to keeping in touch with those who are important to us personally and professionally. We just have to think outside the box for new ways to solve problems. Look at the newly expanded toolbox that we all have at our disposal with wireless communications and computing technologies.

Dick Tracy, Maxwell Smart and Captain Kirk are Alive and Well in the 1990s

Several generations of Americans have grown up with the images of Maxwell Smart whispering into his shoe phone, Dick Tracy chatting it up with his videophone watch, and Captain Kirk and Picard staying in touch with those lightweight, portable, wireless communicators which look suspiciously familiar to Motorola's new Star Tac cellular phone. Well, except for the wireless video portion on the wrist, all the rest already exist and are in use by tens of millions of Americans as we speak. And as an interesting aside, wireless video is not far off. In fact, by the time you read this book it might be on the market too; the technology is already a reality.

Many small businesses are starting to tap into the power of today's wireless technologies. Those that do are getting a head start and are attaining a clear competitive advantage in the marketplace.

Beating Telephone Tag

Telephone tag is one of the biggest productivity-busters in business today. Numerous studies from telephone companies have shown that fewer than two calls in 10 reach their intended party. That means more than 80% of all business calls end up in voice mail or some other message service. This causes more lost productivity and lost business than most entrepreneurs want to admit.

With all of today's basic communications products and services working together, there are no longer excuses for missing another important call. More urgent than that, your business's viability and very survival could depend on your ability to be there when the customer calls, whether you are there or not. It brings new meaning to the question, "Is there a *there*, there?"

Look at what's happening in Hong Kong. Several years ago it was became apparent that it would be in everyone's best interest if everyone carried cheap, lightweight, portable, cellular phones.

That commitment was made and today, if you go over there, everybody is walking around with cellular phones glued to their ears. Sounds funny, but they've virtually eliminated telephone tag.

That gave them a measurable competitive advantage over us and every other more mature country. Many major emerging cities in Asia are the same way. Their phone systems were not much better than tin cans and wires, so new phone networks are mostly wireless, because they're cheap and easy to install compared to their wired counterparts. As a result, every business person carries a cellphone and constantly talks on it no matter where he or she may be. The pulsating energy of the entrepreneurial spirit can be felt on every street corner.

We, on the other hand, have the best phone system in the world. It just happens to be wired. So there has been nothing driving the growth of cellular other than the competitive benefits and convenience it brings over and above traditional hard-wired networks. In other words, having the best network in the world created a delay in our rapid adoption of cellular as an alternative. We had to prove to ourselves it could offer a competitive advantage. It took us several more years, but we finally caught on. Cellphone sales in the United States are now exploding.

"Cellular used to be a status symbol," says *USA Today* reporter Melanie Wells, who covers the frenzied world of advertising. "Today, it's the price of admission. In today's fast-lane business world telephone tag takes its toll, but facing a daily deadline, I can't afford to miss calls." In an age where more than 80% of all business calls end up in telephone tag, cellphones, pagers and other wireless communications and messaging technologies can mean the difference between winning or losing business.

Cutting the Cord

Let's look at today's hottest wireless business technologies. We'll start with the basic tools of the trade—cellphones and pagers. Most people who own a cellphone or a pager use them as stand-alone devices and don't take full advantage of their capabilities. Sure, they are at least right up there with the "better than nothing," but that's not even scratching the surface of the real power these tools offer. Most people don't even leave their cellphones on, or carry them with them. Yet these are the same people who complain of missing calls and losing business opportunities.

After making them as much of a must-have-with-you-at-all-times item as your business cards and a good pen, the trick is using them in conjunction with a variety of other services you can order from your phone company. Used in concert, you'll never have to miss an important call again, unless you want to, of course.

Cellular is White Hot

The first cellular communication system was activated in Chicago on October 13, 1983. According to the Cellular Telecommunications Industry Association (CTIA), AT&T predicted that fewer than 1 million people would use cellular services by the year 2000.

Reality check: As of early 1997, there were roughly 40 million cellular customers, and that number is growing at an annual rate of about 30%. It took 10 years, from 1983 to 1993, to reach the first 10 million customers. In the following three years that number quadrupled to 40 million. In 1997 alone, some 14 million phones are expected to be sold. Small businesses using cellular have a competitive advantage today, but it's quickly becoming a core business tool, like the fax machine.

Are you up to speed with cellular yet? If not you are losing a competitive advantage. According to a Sprint/Roper Small Business Survey, 62% of small businesses use cellular. That still leaves 38% of small businesses at a competitive disadvantage.

Growing a Business with Wireless Technology

Steve Stonely, owner of S&S Landscaping Services, faced a dilemma. His thriving landscaping business was keeping him away from the office for much of the day at various work sites, which was causing him to miss calls and new business opportunities.

Unlike most of his competitors, who continue to struggle with the problem, Stonely turned to technology to keep him connected. With a cellphone in one hand, a shovel in the other and a pager clipped to his belt, he has positioned himself to keep one step ahead of the competition.

"Customers want a live voice when they call—and they want answers. That's why even a live answering service isn't enough for me anymore," says Stonely. This is a trend that seems to be sweeping across all industries. Customers today do seem to be holding businesses to a higher standard of customer service and responsiveness than ever before. Increasingly, if a business can't meet that higher level of customer expectation, your customers will find someone who will.

That's why Stonely armed himself with the tools that enable his customers to reach him wherever he is and whenever they call. When Stonely is out of the office, he uses one of the Call Forwarding services from the local phone company. He has all his calls forwarded to his cellphone, which he keeps clipped to his belt, right next to his pager. The pager is there if his cellphone is out of range or in case the chain saw drowns out the ringing. Simple as is sounds, this solution has helped Stonely increase his business by being there for customers whenever they call. "It's not cheap to use a cellphone and pager this much, but I look at it like this, how much business would I lose by not having it?"

Architect Plans to Stay in Touch

John Draper, an architect, had a similar problem. When he was on job sites, he also had his calls forwarded to his cellphone. But he was still missing calls. Clients who called when he was already on the phone got a busy signal. He tried Call Waiting, but that wasn't appropriate as he kept bouncing between calls, and he felt out of control. So he arranged with his cellular carrier to forward overflow calls to his Voice Mail service. This worked great since clients never got a busy signal.

How did he know when he had messages waiting in Voice Mail? Simple. He programmed the Voice Mail service to dial his pager, of course. By sending a pre-determined code over his pager, he was notified that he had a message waiting and to check his Voice Mail.

Pagers are as Hot as Cell Phones

The number of pagers in use today is roughly the same as cellphones, and they are continuing their own stellar growth pattern. Many new customers use pagers for personal, emergency and safety reasons; however, business customers continue to be the real power users.

Either way, it doesn't much matter who is using the phone or the pager. The point is that more and more of us rely on them to stay in touch. As consumers and business customers depend on the convenience and immediacy of wireless communications, their customer service expectation level continues to rise. They know that staying in touch and being available is part of their lives. They are demanding no less from the people with whom they do business.

Interviews with hundreds of cellular users confirm a growing impatience for and irritation with business contacts who continue to be unreachable. Their logic is simple: "If I use this stuff and can stay in touch, it's not too much to expect the people I do business with to also have that same level of responsiveness to my needs." And the startling thing is, many businesses who continue to do things the way they always did things are at risk of losing this increasingly large customer segment *unless they become as connected as their customers.*

It's the same frustration you experience when calling someone who doesn't own an answering machine. If they aren't home, you can't even leave a message. That leaves the onus on you to keep trying to get through, instead of allowing technology to deliver the message to the party when he returns. Nothing is more frustrating.

Since the cellular explosion has been tracked so closely, most industry analysts are now projecting there will be more than 100 million customers by the year 2000. A far cry from the initial projection of one million customers by then.

Think you don't need cellular? Think everyone in your organization doesn't need cellular? Think your customers aren't getting used to—and beginning to demand—that level of responsiveness? Think cellular is still a toy for the rich, or a tool to stay in touch in case of emergencies, rather than for everyday business communications? Think again. Cellular has become a core business tool for staying in touch with your customers and prospects.

Keep Customers from Bouncing Around

The birthday party for my twins, Adam and Jennifer, was coming up. Since it will be a summer party, my wife and I decided to have a carnival atmosphere. We decided to rent a Moon Walk, one of those giant, inflatable jumping-and-bouncing rooms that active kids love. We found advertisements for several in the back of a kids' newspaper. Surprisingly, competition is pretty heated among businesses that rent Moon Walks. I called one, and their voice mail said they were out and would call us back as soon as they could.

After leaving a message I called the second name on the list. Their voice mail also said they were out, so I left a message. Before the echo died, the phone rang. It was the second business I just called. They had programmed their voice mail to page them when a call came in. After listening to the message, they hit a few buttons and were on the horn with me within minutes. After a few minutes of questions and answers, I placed an order for the inflatable jumping thing. I also was talked into a helium tank and a snow-cone maker. Okay, so I love snow cones.

An hour later, normally an acceptable time frame in yesterday's terms, the first business called me back. They were too late, and they lost a $400 sale because they are still doing things the way they've always done things. Anyway, the party was a hit. My kids invited 60 of their closest friends from the neighborhood and everyone had a great time bouncing around with a snow cone in one hand and a helium balloon in the other. What a scene!

Can't Afford Not to Have it

Many small-business owners tell me they can't afford to have all this technology. They say cellphones, pagers, voice mail, call forwarding, and so on, are just too expensive. They just don't get it. They're thinking about it backwards. Landscaper Stonely hit it right on the button. The question is not how much does this stuff cost? The question is, how much extra business do you get by using it? Even scarier, how much business will you lose by not having these basic communications tools? In most cases, the additional business, or avoided lost business, dwarfs the cost of the technologies.

In the case of the Moon Walks, my $400 order would have bought quite a lot of cellphone and pager time. And, how many other deals are they losing, with no idea what's happening, because many potential customers getting voice mail go to the next name on the list without even leaving a message?

Don't Worry; I Hear that all the Time

Last year we moved. Before closing day I wanted to have the house inspected, so I asked the Realtor for the names of a few inspectors. She gave me two cards. I called the first and got the voice-mail message that they were on an inspection and would call back soon. Sound familiar? So I called the second one and he answered. He too was in the field doing an inspection, but had his calls forwarded to his cellphone, which was clipped to his belt.

After a few minutes of discussion I hired him on the spot. I liked being able to reach him instead of playing phone tag. This was roughly a $500 sale—enough to pay for the cellphone bill for at least a couple of months. A couple of hours later the first inspection service called me back. I apologized, and said I had gone with someone else who had answered right away. The representative responded, "Don't worry, this happens all the time."

I almost hit the floor. *Helloooo!* I was speechless. Wake up, Mr. Fred Flintstone, and smell the coffee. How much business do you have to lose before you catch on? And he was lucky. Potential customers are *telling* him what he needs to do and how much business he is losing. But he's still doing things the same way he's always done things. He's not changing. How long do you think he's got?

This is not—I repeat NOT—a passing fad. This is not even a trend. This is beyond a trend. This is a fundamental change, a permanent transformation in the way business is conducted. A change in the rules of doing business. Ignore the new rules at your own peril!

Wireless Payphones

Some small businesses maintain payphones for the convenience of their customers. Others provide payphones to generate income. Either way, the payphone industry has changed dramatically in recent years. One significant trend is the proliferation of new wireless payphones, made by Nokia and others.

Such phones can be installed quickly almost anywhere, for temporary or permanent service. Just like airphones on airlines, these cellular payphones can be installed in charter buses, limousines, taxis, boats and virtually anywhere you find mobile people with credit cards. They can also be installed temporarily at sporting events, music concerts, county fairs and carnivals.

Wireless Phones Raising the Bar in Retail

Every customer can tell you horror stories of calling a store for information on a product and being put on hold forever, while the person with the answers is being paged or tracked down. She was either busy with another customer or away from her desk (and the wireline phone). Today, retailers are discovering the benefits of cordless.

Whether it's an ordinary cordless phone for the smallest of retail stores, or a fleet of wireless phones tied into the store's PBX phone system, everyone who talks with customers has a phone clipped to his or her belt. You've probably noticed this at stores like Home Depot and Sears, where the sales help is always wandering the floor helping customers. According to store personnel, "Customers don't wait on hold anymore. We get to them wherever we are and whenever they call." This trend in retail is important. Customers are getting accustomed to not waiting on hold anymore; if they are stuck on hold for too long they will vote with their feet.

Untethering of America

Never being out of touch can be good or bad depending on how you handle the technology. Cellphones and pagers can both enslave and liberate you. Used correctly, they can free you to go anywhere, be anywhere, yet never miss an important call. We used to be tied to our offices and homes waiting for important calls. Entrepreneurs frequently missed vacations for fear of being out of touch when needed.

Now, however, with the simple cellphone and pager, you can be anywhere and still be in touch. Many business people have told me they are taking vacations for the first time in years because of this anytime/anyplace revolution. They are attending their kids' ball games and plays in the comforting knowledge that they are only a quiet vibrating page away. I know entrepreneurs who are hitting the golf course again because they can be reached on the links. Sure, it's not as nice as being disconnected altogether (which, by the way, is only the push of the *Off* button away), but at least it allows them to be on the course and away from the office for some well-deserved recreation time.

Okay, we can get carried away. Some people can even take this to ridiculous extremes. We can be taking and making calls anywhere and everywhere and never have a moment's peace. We can be rude and take calls at restaurants and parties and other inappropriate places. But used within reason, and if we remember how to use the *Off* button and how to forward non-important calls to voice mail for later retrieval, these tools will liberate us. Call it the untethering of America. The cutting of the cord. Freedom is contagious, and this technology is setting business people free from coast to coast.

Andrew Seybold, editor of *The Outlook on Communications and Computing*, told *USA Today* that people are becoming more mobile and less attached to their desks. As they become more mobile, he added, they are demanding more mobile communications solutions.

Pagers: Beyond those Annoying Little Beepers, toward Message Centers.

Pagers today are no longer those simple, annoying beepers your father used (if your father was a doctor or a plumber). Now they are full-service message centers that everyone can use for business and family messaging. Forget being limited to simple phone numbers on your screen. Today you can get full text messages—even voice messaging—on your pager, and store them for later review.

You can even get two-way paging and respond to the sender with the touch of a few buttons on your pager. That way, they know you got the message, plus you can answer them, which saves time and money. Look out Dick Tracy, here comes Rich Entrepreneur.

I save the important pager messages that arrive in a personal folder on my pager. The messages could be about getting new business, congratulations on winning an award, and really important ones like, "Dad, I'm sorry I was mean to you. Can I come out of my room now? Love Jason." When my then nine-year-old son called the paging service operator to leave the message, the operator laughed, musing, "Don't you just love the nineties?"

News, E-mail and More on Your Pager

You can get news headlines concerning your industry, or anything else that interests you, sent to your pager twice a day. You can even have your e-mail sent to you by pager so you don't miss an important message. It's saved me from driving across town to cancelled-at-the-last-minute meetings several times, and even caught me, before hopping on an airplane for a cross-country jaunt, to inform me the meeting was postponed. Not only did that message save me two days of travel time, it also saved me a thousand dollars in airfare. No small benefit there.

Service can be city-wide, regional, national or international, depending on your needs. Prices typically vary from $10 to $60 per month, according to the features and coverage, but that's usually a small price to pay to save one deal or close one extra piece of business. And prices are expected to drop even further as new competition keeps bursting onto the scene.

Pest Control Only a Beep Away

With nearly 40 million pagers clipped to belts of all sorts of business people, you'd think that everybody who'd want a pager would already have one. Right? Not necessarily. The president of a $25 million pest-control company, who just purchased 6,000 pagers for his front-line people, lamented, "My business is getting more competitive all the time. My competitors are starting to get a bigger share of the new business because they all have pagers and cellphones and they get back to customers before we do. Pardon the pun, but they're eating us alive. We've got to be more responsive. Increasingly, the first competitor a customer reaches gets the business."

Think this is only happening in the pest control business? This is happening across the board in industry after industry. Even in the sleepiest industries. As long as you've got competition, you've got to keep the edge.

Use It or Lose It

Why don't more small businesses get the most out of these basic tools? Too many use them sparingly. They use their cellphones only for an occasional call. Not many people even know their pager number. This is like using only 10% of our brainpower. Most business people are using only 10% of their technology power.

Put your cellphone and/or pager number on your business cards, your letterhead, your voice mail—everywhere a customer could call you and miss you. If you don't put the numbers everywhere, then make sure you forward all your calls so you can be reached. Make it easier for customers to reach you. Put the onus on yourself. Take my word for it. After interviewing thousands of customers over the years, I know that they won't work very hard trying to reach you. Past a point, they'll try to reach your competition.

Sure, if you use this stuff more it will cost you more. But, if you use it right, along with costing more, it will also save you more (remember my almost-wasted trips) and make you more money because fewer customers will call your competition if they get you first.

Digital: The Next Generation of Wireless

As valuable as the basic cellphone and pager technology can be, the next generation of digital phones is even better, combining the best of all the tools into one handheld device. John Sterling is an East Coast attorney who used to carry a pager and a cellphone, using them together with Voice Mail and Call Forwarding to make sure he didn't miss any calls. Now he carries a new breed of wireless phone that does it all, and then some—a digital wireless phone. Available from a growing number of cellular or PCS providers, it's a combination pager, cellphone, Caller ID, Voice Mail and Call Forwarding system, all in one.

This new technology gives him the power to take control of his communications. Since the phone also acts like a pager, he's able to read incoming e-mail on the phone's screen. General and industry news also is sent over that same screen. And, of course, he's able to get all his regular incoming pages. Then, at the touch of a button, he's able to return the call.

Since not every call is equally important, when a call comes in, Sterling can see who is calling with built-in Caller ID and decide whether to take the call or let it go to Voice Mail. This saves money because, with a cellular phone, you pay for both incoming and outgoing calls. More importantly, it saves time because you no longer feel compelled to take every call.

Voice Mail is usually an integral part of the package. Working at the network level, the voice message is stored and a "message waiting alert" is sent to the phone. That way, he knows when a message is waiting and callers don't have to wait until he gets around to checking his messages. Privacy is another issue today, and, compared to standard analog phones, digital phones make it more difficult for the bad guys to listen in on your private conversations.

Privacy During Telephone Calls is a Gamble at Best

Privacy in wireless communications is becoming a slippery-slope issue and a growing problem. With all the technology on the street in the hands of the bad guys, you can no longer be assured your conversations are private. U.S. Speaker of the House, Congressman Newt Gingrich, learned that lesson the hard way when a private cellular phone discussion became public in a highly publicized case of cellphone snoopers. If it can happen to the third-in-line to the Presidency, it can happen to you and me.

I often forget that others might be snooping in on my conversations. In fact, the proliferation of cellular, cordless, PCS, digital cellular and other assorted wireless phones is making it virtually impossible to be assured a private conversation unless you have expensive scrambling equipment. Even then, it works only when the equipment is connected at both ends. Not the case for the average call.

Executives, thinking they are alone, discuss confidential strategy and trade secrets over cellular phones. Individuals spread gossip, complain about friends or discuss sensitive personal information over cordless phones as though no one is listening. In fact, at any given moment, there are millions of delicate conversations shooting through the airwaves, easily intercepted by anyone with a listening device as sophisticated as a scanner, or as innocent as a baby's nursery monitor.

We have to realize that the days of guaranteed privacy are history. Even if you are using a wired phone, you cannot be assured the party you are talking to is doing the same. As long as one party is wireless, the conversation is vulnerable. And with the continuing explosion of wireless phones, it will only get worse before it gets better. Digital wireless calls are better protected from invading ears, but all this means is that the eavesdropper has to work a little harder. Not a problem for those who do this for a living, or even as a hobby, for that matter.

There are roughly 40 million cellular customers as of 1997. The vast majority are using the original analog cellular service that began life as we know it in Chicago in 1983. Combine this traditional cellular with the tens of millions of cordless phones on the market, and you can easily see the magnitude of the risk to privacy. As long as one party is using cellular or cordless, privacy is no more than wishful thinking.

The industry is counting on the new breed of digital phones to solve the privacy issue. Digital cellular and PCS phones are harder to monitor. Harder, but not impossible. Another entrant in the "better than nothing" category. The only problem is that most digital phones do not work everywhere yet, like cellular phones do. As the digital cellular and PCS continue to roll out market by market, those benefits will become more apparent.

Cellular? Digital Cellular? PCS?
What's the Difference?

Today, there are typically two main cellular carriers in each city: the wireline (usually associated with the local phone company) and the non-wireline (a competing provider, often the cellular arm of another local phone company from another part of the country). Resellers are also moving into many cities, increasing the choices available. But the good news is, before long you'll have six to 10 wireless-telephone providers in each city. That competition should bring the prices down and keep service and features up. Which of these services will be the standard? Cellular, digital cellular, PCS, or one of the other wireless phone networks that are hitting the market? There is no easy answer to this question.

I don't see the wireless wars as a zero-sum game. This will not likely be a VHS vs BETA type war with only one winner. There is no reason why multiple technologies can't thrive in the marketplace. Very likely, multiple choices will remain available since they will all have various strengths and weaknesses. They will be target-marketed toward specific customer groups and their specific needs. Research is finding that customers don't care much which actual technology they use. They just want the features and the functionality. They'll be just as satisfied with a digital cellular phone as a PCS phone as long as it will do what they want it to do.

Cordless phones used at home and in the office allow you to wander around untethered while talking, using a simple, easily-tunable frequency. Just ask anybody with babies how many of the neighbor's interesting cordless conversations they've picked up on their nursery monitor. Often, if close neighbors also have a cordless phone using the same channel, conversations can easily be picked up by each other's phones. Some of today's cordless phones are a little better, with automatic scanning among multiple channels, so you can find the clearest channel available at the moment.

Wireless is going to play an increasingly important role in the future. Just about everyone will be talking on cordless or cellular phones. The new phones will be a hybrid of cordless and cellular. Wireless local telephone service is coming to the marketplace before long. Soon you'll have the choice of using your local phone company's hard wire, or one of the long-distance companies wireless phone services. Either way, you'll be carrying a phone which acts like a cordless phone when you are near your home or office, and automatically converts to a digital cellular or PCS phone when you leave the vicinity.

Read Before Signing the Cellular Contract

You've noticed that cellular telephones are practically given away when you sign up for cellular service. My "free" cellular phone almost cost me $300. That was before Wolf Camera & Video in Atlanta and BellSouth Mobility came to the rescue. My close call should be a lesson to anyone planning to buy a cellphone, whether it's your first or an upgrade.

I've had cellular phones for more than a decade and, like trading in a car every few years, I get the urge to upgrade my phone to the newest, smallest toy every now and then. After an unusually compelling barrage of advertising, I gave in to the itch and bought a new phone. I went to Wolf Camera and Video, one of BellSouth Mobility's authorized agents, and did what I usually do—sign up for another free phone and a two-year plan, cancelling my old phone service.

Several months later, I got a letter from Wolf Camera telling me they were charging my credit card $300 for violating a section of the contract. *Yikes!* Three hundred dollars for a free phone! This must be a mistake, I thought. At first, I was angry; they must be wrong. After all, I'm in the phone business. I should know better. Right? So I pulled out my agreement, read it, and sank into my seat. Now I was angry at *me*. After all, I should know better.

Apparently, there was a new clause which allowed them to charge me if I activated a new line in order to get a free phone, and cancel the existing line—like I'd always done before. In my defense, I had purchased several cellphones in the last 10 years and had never seen this clause before. Yeah, I know; that's no excuse for not reading the contract. But cellphone contracts seem as unnecessarily long as car rental agreements. And, after all, how many frequent travelers read those things every time they rent a car? However, maybe we should from now on. Someday they might slip in a clause that says we get slapped with a $300 penalty for bringing a car back dirty or empty of gas.

To make matters worse, I had visited a few BellSouth Mobility stores and the Wolf Camera and Video store over several days. I explained to all the clerks I met along the way what I wanted to do, but nobody said that was a no-no. Since what happened to me also happened to lots of other customers, the clerks have since been retrained to ensure that customers don't break the rules.

So I was sitting there with this $300 charge, for which I was legally responsible, but since I was so clear about my intentions, without one red flag being raised, I felt a little betrayed. I let my guard down a bit because I was dealing with two companies whom I always trusted. After all, I thought, if there was something wrong with what I said I was going to do, they'd tell me, wouldn't they? This was my reasoning in my letter to Wolf Camera. A couple weeks later a customer service representative called to apologize for the confusion and say that the $300 had been credited back to me.

They didn't have to do it. After all, me and lots of other customers (December was a very busy month for cellphone sales) signed on the dotted line. But Wolf Camera and BellSouth cared so much about their long-term relationships with their clients, they bit the bullet and did the right thing by unsuspecting customers. My hat is off to these two companies. As competition heats up in the cellular marketplace, this is the kind of behavior that companies need to exhibit to keep customers happy. And as things heat up, keeping a customer happy is the only way to keep a customer—period!

Sales Star *WOWs*
Prospects with Technology

While at a conference of small-business owners in Memphis, the owner of a mid-sized firm shared this story. I had just finished discussing a few real-life examples of technology applications, and he was bursting to tell me about his top salesman, who stays that way, the owner said, by being armed to the gills with the latest technology. It's expensive, he said, but a few extra sales pay for the whole shootin' match, and he has easily paid for everything dozens of times over.

He explained that his star salesman would go to an office building or office park and find the company directory. He'd write down names of businesses he wanted to contact, get the phone numbers from the phone book in his car or call Directory Assistance with his cellphone. He'd then call each business to get the name and fax number of the person he needed to contact. Then, he'd plug his notebook computer into his cellphone and, from the front seat of his car, fax off brief notes of introduction to each. He'd include a brief but pertinent article with the fax and then explain that he was in the parking lot and that he'd sent this fax from his car.

He'd then call each to introduce himself and offer to stop by for a brief *hello*. His success rate was astounding, and, he says, he's invited up, on the spot, two out of three times. Of the remainder, many come to the parking lot just to see how he did it!

As management guru Tom Peters says, you've got to *Wow* them. If you look and sound like everyone else, you'll never get past the front door. So think about it. By using all the tools available to you today, how can you *Wow* your customers and prospects?

Cutting Your Laptop's Cords

With only minutes between planes, I desperately needed to send some e-mail before I boarded the next flight, but I couldn't find a phone with a jack to plug in my laptop. That's when I decided to cut the cord and buy a cellular fax/modem. Never again, I thought, would I be caught unable to log-on just because I couldn't find a phone. All you have to do is buy a cellular PCMCIA fax/modem card and you're in business, right? Yeah, right. Sure, everything works great now, but getting from there to here was a journey in frustration. If you have a hankering to cut the cord, let my painful lessons save you some aggravation.

As any road warrior will tell you, the notebook computer is a vital tool for keeping up, so you don't return to a mountain of work back at your office. All you need is a phone line, and you can e-mail, communicate and collaborate with your co-workers, customers and suppliers.

These modems are getting cheaper and faster all the time, and they simply plug into the PCMCIA slots in your laptop. There are also "cellular-ready" and "cellular-capable" versions. Cellular-ready means that it comes with a cable to attach to your cellphone (if you are lucky enough to have the right phone, that is). Cellular-capable means that you have to order the cable for your specific phone. This can take several weeks—if they are in stock. If not, it can take months.

I bought the Megahertz 28.8 with the retractable X-jack, which is as much of a "gotta-have-it" as those little rubber-eraser-type mouse sticks embedded in the middle of laptop keypads made popular by IBM Thinkpads. It came with a cable, which fit my Motorola 550 Flip Phone. I should have been ready to hit the ground running, but that's only if you still believe in the Tooth Fairy.

All modems need a driver to make them work, and even though I have Windows 95, pre-loaded with zillions of drivers, the driver to make my modem work was not there. So I loaded the driver that was included with the kit and, three beeps later, I was connected. So far, so good. After reconfiguring all my communications software and online services to dial into new numbers that run at the higher speeds, I logged on. Using a regular landline phone line, the cellular fax/modems work just fine. Just like an ordinary landline modem. Connecting them to a cellular phone is a different story.

Even with the cleanest and strongest of cellular connections, they slow way down, but at least they work. The frustration comes with a less-than-stellar cellular connection or, heaven forbid, a lousy one. During my learning curve, I lost the connection more times than my blood pressure appreciated.

"Cellular fax modems are built with special enhancers to be able to operate during those fuzzy connections," says Steve Grantham of BellSouth Mobility. "However, to get those enhancers to kick in, you've got to tell the cellular network to use their cellular modems on their end." Now he tells me!

To access the cellular modem pools on the phone company side of the connection, you have to dial into them. This typically means programming a few extra digits such as #DATA or *DATA into your dialing software. Call your cellular company for instructions on data cellular calling. Once I found this little secret, life got a whole lot easier, and I lost fewer connections. But it's still not even close to the reliability and speed of a regular land line.

Don't bother trying a cellular connection while moving. The variation in signal strength and the handoff between cells are all that's needed to lose the cellular/data connection. So forget about trying to log on from the back seat of a taxi, unless you are stuck in traffic and not moving. Use your cellular phone signal-strength meter to find the best spot with the strongest connection before you try to log on, and then stay put to increase the likelihood of success with less frustration.

Once everything is set up properly, you may still have to play with it for a while to work out the idiosyncrasies of your particular communications software. Sometimes using your software to dial works best. Other times, manual dialing is better. Manual dialing is when you dial through the phone keypad, instead of using your software, and then connect through your software.

PIN codes raise their own challenges. Cellular phone companies are implementing PIN codes as a cellular fraud deterrent. After dialing the number you are calling and pressing *SEND*, you then hear two quick rings, then silence. To complete the call you must enter your PIN code and press *SEND* again. This can play havoc with any automatic-dialing software program. Manual dialing is usually the best way to go here.

There are many hassles, to be sure, and the technology is still young. But the technology will improve. For those who travel, there is nothing more important than staying in touch, and these cellular modems, as frustrating as they are, will allow you to do just that. Stay connected on the information skyway.

Wireless Modems Save the Day

All of the sudden there is a flurry of activity in computer stores. Road warriors are lining up to get wireless PCMCIA modems. They plug into your notebook computer's PCMCIA slot and enable you to connect to your cellular or wireless service without having to juggle a cellphone in the mix. Some services allow users to leave their notebook receiver on continuously, notifying the owner when mail or information comes in.

Wireless and Laptops, the Next Generation

Laptops work much better with a digital connection compared to the relatively old-fashioned analog cellular. As more cellular systems go digital, and as more wireless digital services are rolled out nationwide in coming months and years, three things will happen.

First, the ability to use computing devices will improve dramatically as ease-of-use and reliability issues are settled. Second, the number of people using these data-centric devices will swell. Third, new and ingenious kinds of handheld and portable computing devices will explode onto the scene because the universe of customers will grow dramatically, making it an increasingly viable marketplace.

No More Meter Readers

Remember when meter readers had to walk up to each home to read electric and gas meters attached to the outside walls? Today, all they have to do is drive through the neighborhood. The meters automatically transmit the necessary information, wirelessly over the airwaves, to a receiver on the meter reader's vehicle. He never needs to get out of his vehicle. This simple wireless technology has improved the efficiency of this task enormously by allowing personnel to cover a lot more ground in the same amount of time. And no more confrontations with cantankerous canines!

Overnight delivery services, like FedEx and UPS, are also using wireless technology to keep track of the exact position of any package through wireless handheld and vehicle-mounted devices. This gives them the control and responsiveness their customers demand today.

Actually, FedEx and UPS are perfect illustrations of competitive forces at work. FedEx developed a huge edge over UPS with its wireless tracking technologies. It was so successful, and such an advantage, that UPS spent a small fortune developing and installing its own system in order to stay competitive. Now they both offer state-of-the-art wireless tracking, and the playing field is once again level. Apparently, wireless technologies were worth billions of dollars in business, enough for UPS to spend a fortune catching up. Something to learn here.

Increase Sales Orders Over the Airwaves

Most businesses are driven by sales. Traditionally, the salesperson has to go out on calls and return the office to do the paperwork and submit the order. Today, smart companies are using wireless data services to allow sales reps to tap into the company's inventory lists, check stock, place orders and confirm the transaction—all right from the customer's office.

Marc Greenspan, owner of an office supply and paper distributorship, has tapped this technology. "Our sales reps do everything from the customer location now. This means that we can take care of the customer on the first visit. Not only do our orders get processed in half the time, but this striking-while-the-iron-is-hot selling has allowed us to close more borderline sales, which, before, often slipped through our fingers because the customer had plenty of time to change his mind before the sales rep could get back with an answer to his question."

If your business requires you to personally visit your customers for sales or service, or even to perform the equivalent of reading their meters (like measuring how many *watzergs* were consumed in the *watzergrater*), then this technology can be a real powerful tool. These services are available from cellular and wireless providers like BellSouth's new Cellemetry service, Ardis, and Ram Mobile Data (*www.ram.com*).

Technology is Changing Real Estate Business

Considered a leader among his colleagues for his use of technology to do more business, REMAX agent Eric Von Kursteiner told *Wireless* magazine that he carries his laptop whenever he goes on calls with clients. He pulls up calendars, schedules, home sale statistics, contract language, and so on. He also uses his cellphone regularly, often to get Multiple Listing Service (MLS) information on properties in his area. However, when asked if he uses the laptop to wirelessly tap into the MLS database, he says, "I'm not quite there yet." I'll bet dimes to donuts that Von Kursteiner will be there before too long.

This is a huge opportunity for the real estate community, or any other business that is information intensive, for that matter. Most agents are still using cellphones and pagers, but only a handful are bringing laptops into the field, which they load up each morning with pictures and information on homes their clients would be interested in learning about. But a few of today's cutting-edge high-producers are just starting to cut the cord and wirelessly link their laptops to the MLS database or other data services—downloading all the information they need to do business wherever they are located, without having to go back to the office or find a phone line. This allows them to accomplish more work and to serve clients in ways most other agents only dream about.

Pampering Customers

There are many ways to leverage the power of pagers and cellphones. Don't simply think in terms of keeping in touch with your customers. Think also of creative ways to improve your business, and your customer's experience doing business with you.

For example, busy, cutting-edge restaurants today hand out pagers to customers who are waiting to be seated. Instead of announcing names on a loudspeaker, they quietly page diners when their tables are ready. This allows those waiting the chance to slip the surly bonds of the restaurant lounge or crowded front-door area and take a little stroll or window-shop in the vicinity. This service also alleviates the ambiance-busting roll-call announcements: "Smith, party of four, your table is ready!" Customers love this. It's different, and it says, "I care about your experience," which matters in today's increasingly competitive markets.

Cutting the Umbilical Cord

Why stop there? Don't limit yourself to thinking of how to integrate telecommunications into your business. Why not think of new businesses that use telecommunications? Think of a new twist on an old problem. The Umbilical Cord Company had a great idea, according to the *Atlanta Business Chronicle*. Tapping into every parent's need to stay in touch with their kids, the company embarked on a new business, marketing pagers to parents.

Did Atlanta need another pager company? If you asked me before I heard about Umbilical Cord, I would have said no. But successful businesses are built on ideas and win with marketing. Finding a niche that everyone else is ignoring, and then pouncing on it. That's what Umbilical Cord did. It markets to expecting parents, so dad is never more than a beep away when mom goes into labor.

Incidentally that's how I first got hooked on pagers. I signed up for my first, basic, tone-only beeper three weeks before the due-date for our firstborn, and I haven't taken it off since. Well, not exactly. I've upgraded several times, to where now I have a state-of-the-art text pager that sends me full messages wherever I am located in the United States. It's a comforting feeling knowing you are only a page away in case your family or your business need you. At those moments, and there are plenty of them, pagers are worth their weight in gold.

The Umbilical Cord Company also markets its pagers to growing families. In our increasingly mobile society, in which parents are working and kids are at school or involved in after-school activities, pagers are an increasingly popular way to stay in touch and reach each other. They provide peace of mind that parents didn't have before. Knowing they can reach out and touch their kids with a beep—to have them call or simply get their rear ends back home, already.

Whatever you think about the state of our society, when parents use pagers to keep in touch with their kids, you've got to admit an idea like the Umbilical Cord Company is right on-target. And, there are plenty of great ideas like this one just waiting to be realized. Just think of everyday situations and problems faced by a market segment, like families in this case, and think how some of today's new technology can solve old problems in new ways. Plenty of great ideas, like this one, will be hits. One of them might just as well be yours.

When Traveling, Take Your Cell Phone and Keep Your Travel Agent's Number Handy

If your plane experiences mechanical problems and you are forced to deplane, unless you are first out the door, you will find yourself in a long line that forms instantly at the gate's ticket counter, and also at every nearby payphone. Everybody wants to get re-booked on another flight. Those precious minutes often determine who gets those last seats on the only other flight scheduled for that evening.

Grabbing your cellphone and calling your travel agent can get you re-booked within minutes. This has saved my tail many times. Even if you ignore all the other obvious benefits of a cellphone, it would still be worth having just to help you leapfrog over some of life's more aggravating Maalox moments.

Technology Lets You Get Away from the Office

Being plugged into the electronic village means never having to say you're sorry you're away on vacation and can't be reached. Notebook computers, e-mail, faxing, and news and information services are becoming basic tools of business. The good, or bad, part—depending on your perspective—is that they go wherever you go.

This might not be good news, if you're an overworked employee who doesn't want to hear from your boss or your customers when you're on vacation, in which case you can choose to leave these toys behind. But for business owners, managers and employees, who typically scale back or even cancel vacation plans because they can't afford to be out of touch, the benefits of the technology are all good. Increasingly, technology is enabling people to take vacations or take a day off, to go fishing for the first time in years.

We took the kids to the beach for a few days of sun and surf. As a small-business owner, I had to stay in touch with the news, my clients and associates. So I schlepped along my trusty IBM Thinkpad, loaded with my e-mail communications and information software, and my cellphone and pager. You might have thought I was off on a business trip, but the truth is that business people, myself included, think twice about going away because our business requires timely responses and staying in touch. Something you can't easily do while basking in the sun on the beach. Until now.

The lines between the office and home, and between work and play, are blurring. More and more people are working from home part-time or all of the time. And, this revolution is not limited to working from home. You can work from anyplace. Executives often tell me that they work while on a plane, in a hotel, a client's office, a library, or even while sitting in their car before meetings.

Regi Campbell, President and CEO of InterServ, says he often arrives early at meetings so he can spend some quiet time working in the car. In that hour or so, away from distractions of the office, he often accomplishes more in one hour than in an entire morning at the office. That's how the power of the technology is changing the way we work.

While away, with my notebook computer, I am able to read what's going on back home by logging on to Access Atlanta, the online edition of the *Atlanta Journal and Constitution* newspaper. Many major newspapers have online editions. I am also able to stay in touch with the national news, and get all the news about my industry, via online services and the Internet. I also receive important e-mail messages from clients to whom I need to respond. These are messages I used to have to stay in the office to handle. Now, all I have to do is hit *REPLY*, answer a few questions, attach a few files, hit *SEND*, and the correspondence is complete. No stationery, stamps or mailbox necessary, and they have their replies in minutes, not days.

Peter Keene takes anytime/anyplace communications to new heights. The telecom columnist and consultant decided to pack up and move his business to a home office in the Caribbean. He's able to conduct business as usual, while gazing at a gorgeous panoramic view of crystal blue waters. Anytime/anyplace communications can be truly liberating. Don't limit yourself. It can change the way you live and work. It gives you choices. The choice to work where you want, when you want. The point is that we have many tools at our disposal to help us keep in touch with our families, customers, suppliers and associates. And, most of us don't use them to their fullest advantage. They can either liberate or enslave us, depending on how we use them. Used correctly, they can represent the untethering of America. No longer are we chained to our desks or homes. We can go anywhere and still stay in touch—and do business just like we were back at the office.

Mobile and Wireless Tips:

Extra Batteries
Always keep a stash of extra batteries for everything. There's nothing more frustrating than having a phone with dead batteries. Lots of people have Motorola Flip Phones. Motorola has a neat new battery pack. It's an empty shell of the battery pack. You load

it with six AA Alkaline batteries and you're in business. Batteries run out? Forget charging it. All you have to do is pull out a few extra AAs and you're back in touch.

Buying Cellular

Buying cellular phones doesn't have to be difficult. There are two decisions: the service and the phone. The service comes from a variety of vendors. Historically there were two main carriers in each town: the wireline (typically a unit of the local phone company) and the non-wireline (typically a unit of an out-of-region local phone company). That has changed to where AT&T, MCI, Sprint and others now offer cellular and wireless phone services. There are typically six to 10 wireless phone companies in each major city, or there will be soon. Plans vary, so determine the best plan for you based on how much you use the phone. If you are new to cellular, go for the basic service and a short-term plan. Then make changes in plans as you determine your usage patterns.

The phone is the other part. Installed car phones or portable bag phones have typically three watts of power, which provide better reception and more reliable communications than the pocket-size phones. But they are not as portable. Handhelds can go anywhere, but have only .5 watts of power. This is so you don't fry your brains, and keeps them small in size. The reduction in power, however, carries a price. It suffers from a noticeably noisier connection, and erratic handoffs between cell towers as you are moving. More dropped calls are also a problem.

Despite the handheld's shortcomings, the point of cellular is *portability*. Anytime/anywhere communications. With that in mind, a car phone or a bag phone, even though they deliver better quality, have their limitations. If you can get both, do so. If you can get only one, get a good handheld.

Scam: Don't Touch that Pager!

If you get a mysterious page asking you to call a number in area code 809, DON'T! This is probably a scam. This area code covers the Caribbean region. The scam is based on a pay-per-call deal.

The number you are asked to call is a pay-per-call number, like a "900" number, except that you don't know it in advance. In fact, you won't know it until you get your phone bill. By simply calling the number, you immediately incur huge fees which later show up on your phone bill. And it's getting even more complicated, because more than a dozen Caribbean countries were assigned new area codes in 1997. Watching out specifically for 809 calls may no longer be enough after 1997.

Get PINned

Cellular fraud is costly and invasive. When you are talking on your cellphone, pirates using high-tech listening devices pick your cellular ID out of thin air and use it to reprogram other cellphones to your ID. They sell these hot-wired phones to drug dealers, immigrants, or anyone who can't afford full phone service or doesn't want to be traced. You find out when you get a huge phone bill—sometimes for thousands of dollars.

PIN numbers are a good defense. Personal Identification Numbers are typically a four digit code you must dial before the call can be completed. This makes it more difficult for cell thieves to capture usable numbers out of the air. Not impossible, just more difficult.

So sign up with your cellular phone company for PIN numbers to at least have a fighting chance.

Choosing Among a Multitude of Service Providers

Not only are there many plans and features to choose from, but there's also a growing number of service providers. All the Baby Bells, AT&T Wireless, MCI Cellular and Paging, Sprint Cellular and Paging, and other long-distance companies offer a wide variety of cellular, digital cellular and PCS services. There are also other wireless companies like NEXTEL, which uses a different technology altogether. Its phones act like cellphones, but also act like radios, able to conference multiple users in one call. Also,

Energy giant Southern Company has launched SouthernLinc, which makes its wireless phone network available to business customers. NEXTEL and SouthernLinc both are digital, and have good quality, but their availability is limited to the cities where they have service, and the roaming capabilities are not as universal as cellular, yet.

Chapter 4
Making Money with
Phone Company Services

On September 3, 1996, a *Wall Street Journal* article headline shouted, "Baby Bells Profit By Tapping Phone Paranoia." The article was about all the new services that local phone companies offer to meet every need and concern. What it didn't focus on is how those same services can be used in business to gain an advantage.

The article featured a customer who uses a formidable arsenal of phone services, including one feature that continuously dials a busy number until it gets through, then it rings her back. Another blocks calls from certain numbers, like obscene callers. Another lets only certain calls get through. Another will trace a call. Another will dial back the number of the last person who called. Another is distinctive ringing for certain people so she knows who's calling by the ring pattern. And this is only the tip of the iceberg of available phone company services.

Not only are local, long-distance and wireless telephone companies a wealth of information on the many tools you need to succeed, they also offer many of those services themselves. But they don't just offer services; they offer solutions.

Since you are already their customer, you can hit the ground running. Use your telephone companies to your advantage. They are a resource you can't afford to ignore. If your phone company is not on the cutting edge, offering you a variety of these tools and technologies, it is time to find one that is.

Fortunately, the phone companies no longer focus on just one core area. The days of the plain-old phone company are over. They are not only going through an evolution, but also a revolution, becoming full-service providers offering everything from local and/or long-distance telephone services to cellular, paging and other wireless voice and data services, Internet access and hosting services, e-mail, voice mail, and an ever-increasing list of other services.

June Langhoff wrote a terrific reference book titled *Telecom Made Easy* (Aegis, 1997), which gives a detailed description of the many services phone companies offer. It's also loaded with phone numbers and addresses of assorted resources. My intention here is not so much to describe these services as it is to look at how companies are using them to make money in their business. Pick up a copy of her book to answer questions and get more details about particular services. It's a good all-around telecom primer.

In this chapter you will also read about advanced services that are only beginning to hit the market. Don't despair if your phone company doesn't yet offer all the services described here, because it's only a matter of time before they will become widely available.

The Battle of the Bundle

All of a sudden, you can get several of the services you need under one roof. It's called bundling, and it's the newest rage. Fueled by customer demand, phone companies are offering bundles of products and services.

We have been forced, over the last decade or so, to deal with different companies for various communications needs. We've dealt with separate firms for local, long-distance, cellular, paging, Internet access, e-mail, and so on. Not only that, but we have to deal with different people, call different customer-service numbers, get different bills, and we have to send different checks to each. What a management handful. This has not been a lesson in efficiency, to say the least. Thank goodness this is changing.

Today, you can get many of these services from one company, and before long, you'll be able to get all of them, and more, because new services are being rolled out all the time. Bundling offers many advantages. One is *convenience*. You have one number to call to place an order for several services. You have one number to call for customer service. Another advantage is *cost*. There are usually incentives to bundle services together. Incentives like all the usage counting toward a volume discount. Or special discounts when you order more than one service. Then there's the advantage of *efficiency*—getting one bill and writing one check each month.

The goal of the Telecommunications Act of 1996 was to break down the barriers and allow all the telephone and communications companies into each other's businesses. It's working. Slowly, but it's working.

Term Plans: To Sign or not to Sign; That is the Question

Term plans are another hot issue today. Should you sign a long-term plan or not? That is the question, and this is the dilemma. It is clear that signing term plans with a phone company offers added benefits, both tangible and intangible. However, customers are increasingly concerned about being locked out of the benefits and services that the new competition, when it arrives, will bring. Valid concern. Look at it from both sides and it might make the decision easier.

We are seeing a move in the cellular marketplace away from long-term commitments toward month-to-month deals. Some companies are also moving toward offering loyalty-based programs to keep customers without contracts. Sprint's Fridays Free is a good example. It offers free calling on Fridays. This is an incentive to keep customers long-term without signing term plans. And while this might be the wave of the future, today's reality is that you get more benefit by signing a term plan than by not doing so.

There are extra discounts, special promotions, special offers, special programs, special attention, and all sorts of incentives to sign term plans. Loyalty begets loyalty. In today's marketplace if you show commitment to a phone company, it reciprocates that commitment. Phone companies are reluctant to spend a lot of time, energy and resources with a customer if that customer can pick up and leave tomorrow. Maybe the marketplace will change, but for now these are the realities. So there is real benefit to signing a term plan. But what about the risk? What about the new competition bursting out all over? What about the fear of being locked into a plan and not being able to take advantage of new services and plans?

Valid questions. Let's look at them. First, while there is little doubt that competition will indeed break out all over, it hasn't happened yet. It will take some time. At least a few years. Local and long-distance companies are going through the agonizingly slow regulatory and legal process of getting into each other's business. True, a few competitive services are being introduced in certain markets and for certain customer types. By no means is there real, across-the-board, substantive choice and competition between the local and long-distance companies. When there is, there might be a valid concern about signing a wide-ranging, long-term plan. By that time, there might also be additional benefits to doing so. There might also be term plans addressing only certain aspects of your communications needs. We'll cross that bridge when we come to it.

All the major phone companies are planning to be in each other's businesses and offering each other's services, so you won't be locked out of new services even if they pop up before your plan expires. Most term plans allow you to add or change your services and plans as long as you stay a customer. So, for today, if you are predisposed to signing a term plan for the extra benefits, then don't let the prospect of change and pending competition stop you from realizing real benefits right now. Remember the old adage about a bird in the hand?

Your Phone Company Can Help You *Make* Money, Not Just *Save* Money

The phone companies are in a very competitive marketplace. Use this to your advantage. Demand added value. Look to them as a resource, as a kind of high-tech partner. Call them in to help you analyze your business needs and to make recommendations on services and products that not only help you solve your business problems, but also make money. That's right. *The phone companies can actually help you increase sales as well as decrease expenses.* They can help you make money, if you work closely with them to that end.

Phone company employees work with millions of other small businesses every day. Their customer-service representatives share stories with one another, and because of this, they have a wealth of ideas for your business. They see what other companies are doing—right and wrong—and often can give you money-saving and money-making ideas you would never think of on your own.

They can also draw on their own experience, because the phone companies themselves practice what they preach (most of them anyway). They spend hundreds of millions of dollars to arm their sales and service forces with all the latest tools such as laptops, communications and information software, cellular phones, pagers, e-mail, wireless modems, Intranets, and everything else they need to do business anytime/anyplace.

Let's take a look at some of the more popular and effective phone company services for small businesses. This is by no means meant to be a complete list, but it's enough to get your juices flowing and give you some ideas to implement yourself.

Tip: Do yourself a favor and stay in close touch with your customer reps. They will be happy to keep you up-to-date on new offerings as they are introduced. They'll also help you analyze your needs at regular intervals, and figure out exactly what you should be using and how you should be using it to get maximum advantage and value. It's a win/win relationship for everyone. They get a loyal customer; you get the expertise you need to save money and make money.

Using Caller ID to Stay Close to Customers

Like all small-business owners, Jane Callaway was trying to build customer satisfaction by getting closer to her customers, encouraging reorders and repeat orders. "Saving money by reducing the time on the phone with each customer would be a nice side benefit, too, as long as it doesn't interfere with building customer relationships," Callaway says. She runs a thriving mail-order business and cares as much about generating first-time customers as she does about creating an atmosphere that encourages repeat customers. Her goal is to realize additional and ongoing revenues from her existing customer base. Caller ID enables her to accomplish this goal.

Larger companies have used CTI (Computer Telephony Integration) for years. It was always very equipment-intensive and expensive. Thanks to new technologies, small businesses can now benefit from the same customer relationship building power. Using Caller ID on Callaway's local lines and ANI (Automatic Number Identification) on her 800 lines, the customer telephone number is instantly captured and cross-referenced against her computer database of customers. In the blink of an eye, if it is an existing customer calling to reorder, the number is recognized and the customer's record pops up on-screen for the operator to offer a personal greeting like, "Hello Mr. Smith; thank you for calling;

how may we help you?" By the way, this CTI function is also called a "screen pop" by industry insiders.

Sounds great doesn't it? A personalized greeting. Getting close to the customer. This is exactly what all the management gurus have been telling us to do for years. A side benefit is that this saves precious seconds per call by instantly pulling up customer records. Since time is money in phone services, this saves lots of money, too. *Imagine saving many seconds per call on thousands of calls.*

The only problem was that her customers were caught off guard and were frankly stunned by being greeted by name before even identifying themselves. This proved to be more than the average customer could comprehend—perhaps a little big-brotherish. Callaway spent so much time explaining how she knew the identity of customers that the calls wound up taking *longer* than ever before. So while she still uses this marketing tool, she doesn't let on about it to her customers. She answers the phone with the same old cheery greeting as before, but minus the customer name, even though in roughly two-thirds of the cases she has the name right in front of her.

Now she reports a reduction in the time per call, which saves her company money and provides a more immediate response to callers by having instant access to previous ordering information. Customers are asked how they liked the last item ordered, shipping information is confirmed, and topics discussed during the previous call are touched upon. This tweaking of technology allows Callaway to get closer to her customers, build loyalty, and make more money at the same time.

The moral of this story? There are many, but the most obvious is that technology alone isn't the answer. Technology alone is only a tool, and is no more the answer to building customer relationships than a hammer or a saw is to building a house. Sure, it's a necessary tool if used properly, but if used poorly, it can cause more harm than good. So don't just buy it and install it. Stay close to it and make sure it's doing the job you intended it to do.

Call in to your own business now and then. Play the customer. See what your customers have to deal with—from when the call is answered until it's concluded. Judge the technology, the ease of use, the personnel, and the entire customer experience. You might be shocked into making some immediate changes.

Enhanced Fax Services

Phone companies have started offering a variety of enhanced fax services. These are some of the most powerful tools in business today:

Fax Overflow Mailboxes

What happens when your customer is trying to send you a fax, but you are already getting or sending a fax at the time. That's right: the dreaded busy signal, which is frustrating for customers. Why can't you simply forward those calls to a fax mailbox, like a voice mailbox, for later retrieval? That way, at least, your customer isn't getting upset. The onus is on you, where it should be, not on your customer.

That's exactly what's available today. Many phone companies are beginning to offer this valuable service to their customers. It's a simple process of combining Call Forwarding, Busy Signal with a fax mailbox. When you are traveling, you can even program the service to send all your faxes to the fax mailbox for retrieval by you from wherever you are located.

Jonathan Taylor is an independent consultant who travels frequently on business. "I used to get back to my office only to find important faxes piled up on my fax machine. I could be gone for days at a time. Some of those faxes needed immediate attention, but my absence caused embarrassing delays. Fax mailboxes have definitely come to my rescue. Now, whenever I travel, I forward my fax line to my fax mailbox service. I can retrieve faxes anywhere, anytime, and from any fax machine I happen to be near, whether it be at a client location, hotel, or even one of those fax kiosks at the airport."

Fax Broadcast

Previously available only from stand-alone fax computers or service bureaus, this service is now available from your local and long-distance phone companies. *Fax broadcast* can send your fax to thousands of locations simultaneously. Whether you are a restaurant faxing tomorrow's daily specials to local offices all over town, or whether you fax a newsletter or announcement to the same group of offices or fax machines on a regular basis, fax broadcast services can be a real time and money saver.

The Albacore Ristorante takes advantage of the power of advanced fax services. It has a fax mailing list of regular patrons who appreciate being able to check the daily specials. The restaurant faxes a daily menu and list of specials to about 400 area offices. The result is not only increased dining traffic within the restaurant itself, but also a three-fold increase in the take-out and delivery business in the year following the introduction of the fax broadcast service.

Sterling Accounting has also tapped the power of fax. It faxes tax updates to all its clients on a quarterly basis. This not only provides valuable information to its clients, but it also exposes the firm and its services to its clients on a regular basis—for a very low cost compared to the printing and mailing costs of traditional newsletters. "The only cost is the price of a local phone call to our clients," says owner Alex Sterling. "But the results are astounding. Retention of clients has increased year over year. We have the lowest level of client turnover than ever before. This is money in the bank to my firm."

Fax-on-Demand

Fax-on-demand is also a 24-hour customer-service tool. It allows customers to call in and retrieve any of the frequently-requested documents you've scanned into the system—brochures, menus, price sheets, product information, directions, and so on. Chapter 5 covers fax-on-demand in more detail.

Back to Basics

As small businesses grow, they are ordering extra phone lines in record numbers. In fact, that's one of the reasons we are running out of phone numbers and are seeing new area codes being rolled out all over the country.

As businesses grow, they hire people. Then customers start complaining about not being able to get through because the phone line is always busy, and workers are always waiting in queue for a free line to make an outbound call. So what do most small businesses do? Call the phone company and get a few more lines installed, of course. While that is the right answer, simply ordering the lines is not enough—having them set up the right way is also important, and can make all the difference in the world.

That's what happened to Guy Springfield, whose contracting business was growing, requiring additional phone lines because customers complained of busy signals. But since he didn't order a rollover feature, the problem wasn't solved. "When I finally called to my phone company and complained that things weren't any better, this customer rep finally asked the key question: why didn't I have the lines rollover?" says Springfield. "Why? Because nobody suggested it. Well, that's all it took. Now that the bottleneck is busted, my customers can get through, and everybody's happy."

When ordering extra lines, it's often a good idea to link them together in a rollover, rotary group, or hunt group. Many names, same function. It simply means that the incoming calls go to the first line first. Then, if that line is already busy, the call rolls over to the second line, and so on. Too many businesses simply add lines, don't add them to the rollover, and then don't understand why customers still complain about busy signals. Without a rollover or hunt group, it doesn't matter if you have one line or 10. Without rolling over as soon as the first line is busy, that's it, the game is over; the next incoming call reaches a busy signal, even though you might have nine available lines in waiting.

What Happens When You are on the Line and Another Call Comes in?

Your local phone company has several new calling features that use advanced Call Forwarding and Messaging to handle a common problem—namely, what happens when you are on your line, and another call comes in?

Larger business have multiple lines, automated attendants, voice mail and a wide array of solutions. But until recently, small businesses were stuck with the choice of either the effective, but annoying, Call Waiting, or letting the second caller get a busy signal.

Now there are several Call Forwarding features that, for a few dollars per month, will automatically forward the second call if you are already on the line, or after a pre-selected number of rings if you don't pick up. Here's a brief description of each:

❐ *Call Forwarding, Standard:* Simply sends all calls to another phone line you've selected.

❐ *Call Forwarding, Busy Signal:* Forwards all calls to the number you've selected only when you are on the line, so the customer doesn't have to hear a busy signal or deal with Call Waiting.

❐ *Call Forwarding, No Answer:* Forwards a call after a pre-determined number of rings, to another designated line or to the Voice Mail service provided by the phone company.

Nelson Travel Agency often found itself unable to handle the flow of calls when an airline would suddenly advertise a special travel deal. "Our phones would overload quicker than a swollen river in springtime," says owner David Nelson. With the assorted Call Forwarding services we use from the local phone company, we never miss a call. Every call is either answered or gets forwarded to our Voice Mail service." These services, a must for any small business, help immeasurably in managing your calls and assuring that your callers never reach a busy signal.

What if the incoming call is more important than the call you're already on? Let's say you are talking with your spouse about something that can wait, when the call you've been waiting for all day finally comes in. With Caller ID Deluxe service, combined with Call Waiting, you can see the name and number of the new incoming call. You can then decide whether to hit the *flash* key and take the new call or let it go to the phone company's Voice Mail service.

Expand into New Market Areas Without a Physical Presence

Remote Call Forwarding allows you to offer a local phone number in any city in the country. When a customer calls in to that local number, the call is forwarded to your location, wherever that may be.

Darlene Sanders owns a flower shop in New York, but she has local numbers all over the country. When, say, a Florida customer calls their local number in the Orlando Yellow Pages, they actually reach Sanders in her New York store. In this way, businesses all over the country have found that they can tap whole new markets with only the cost of advertising and having the Remote Call Forwarding phone service.

Everybody Needs a Phone, Not a Phone Line

If you are a very small business, you probably have only a few lines and a simple multi-line telephone system. If you are a bit larger, with more employees and a PBX (private branch exchange) phone system, your needs will be different. One mistake business people make is thinking that they need a phone line for every person. While that might be true for a very small shop, it's not efficient for anything more than a few lines. True, everyone in a business might need a phone on their desk, but they don't need their own dedicated phone line.

An example: Johnson's Nursery does a booming business with area landscapers. It has 20 workers, but only four lines. All 20 phones in the office are wired into the PBX. Four actual phone lines from the phone company are wired into the PBX. The PBX, no more than a computer that acts like a mini-phone company switching station, is the traffic cop.

When one of Johnson's employees picks up one of the 20 phones and tries to get a local line, typically by dialing "9" first, the PBX senses that attempt and connects the caller to one of the four outgoing phone lines. This continues until four phones and all four phone lines are in use. The fifth caller would get a fast busy signal, which means that all lines are in use. It's okay for occasional *busies* to occur during the busy hour of the day, but this shouldn't happen all day long. If it does, it might be time to add a few more phone lines.

Once a Year Traffic Study

It's a good idea once a year to call your local phone company and order a *line and traffic study* to see how much traffic is on each line. It will show you all sorts of interesting management information, including how many calls each line made or received. Once in a while, it will even show lines that aren't working. This can be a real money-saver.

Typically, the first line in a rollover has the most usage, which drops with each successive line. However, you might find that some lines at the end of the rollover have very little usage, or even no usage at all. Little usage might mean you are "overtrunked," and that you are paying for more than you need. Might be time to remove a few lines.

If there is no usage on the lines, you might have a case where you have the lines and are paying for them, but they are not connected to the PBX or phone equipment properly. If you can use the lines, hook them up. If you haven't noticed any bottlenecks, cancel them and save the money. It's really that simple. Johnson's Nursery found all of the problems just mentioned, fixed the inefficiencies, and saved thousands of dollars a year in the process. Not a bad payoff.

Local Service Competition

We've been hearing about the escalating competition for local phone services. Long-distance companies are probably going to be the local phone companies' biggest competitors for local phone service. However, you can expect wireless firms, CAPs (Competitive Access Providers), CLECs (Competitive Local Exchange Carriers), cable TV companies, and even power and gas companies, to get into the action to one extent or another.

Don't expect a complete set of competitive local service offerings right out of the gates. It won't happen overnight, but it will happen. In fact, it's happening now. AT&T, MCI, Sprint and many other long-distance companies are reselling the services of the local phone companies, or offering local services on their own networks. These services will start out being available only to certain market segments, like business customers, and initially only in certain cities or states. Then, as the months go by, more and more people will have access until, eventually, local services will be available everywhere from a wide variety of vendors for residential and business customers of all sizes.

This is the way it happened with long-distance competition, which began in 1984, and it's the same way it will unfold in local service competition. The time-frame will be shorter, but it will still take time to unfold and develop. Most companies, large or small, will not switch all their local services with one sweeping gesture. They will experiment with it, ordering some local services here and there to supplement their existing services. Then, as the comfort level grows, more and more lines and services will migrate to the new carrier. Then, when the customer is comfortable with the level of service from the new providers, the choice will be like that between long-distance providers today.

What's Good for the Goose...

As soon as local competition is up and running, the local phone companies will get into long distance. They are already beginning to offer long distance outside their home regions, and will offer in-region long distance as soon at the FCC says the local markets are sufficiently open to outside competition. What does all this mean for you? Good news. The phone companies will have to fight to win or retain your business. That fight will have only one clear winner: you, the customer.

Centrex

Many business customers want the benefits, features and functionality of a PBX, but prefer not to make a significant capital outlay by purchasing or leasing the equipment. Not only that, but regular maintenance is also quite a commitment of time, technical expertise and money. Then, what do you have to show for it? A system that is outdated as soon as it's installed, just like every other computer-oriented item we purchase. Today's cutting-edge gadget becomes tomorrow's doorstop.

An alternative is using the phone company's network as your own private branch exchange. Enter Centrex services. This is a generic name for a service offered by most local phone companies. The logic is simple. They sell you "smart lines" that are linked directly into their huge computer system.

To you and your employees, the features are the same as having your own PBX, but instead of having the PBX on your premises, the power lies in the intelligence at the network level. All you have in your office are phones. No expensive PBX equipment to maintain, update and upgrade. All that is done by the phone company.

You are left with all the features and functionality that you want—without the headaches and cost of the equipment. "It's a no-brainer for my company," says Steve Miller, who owns an electrical distributorship. "It costs me about the same as plain-old local phone lines, but it does everything an expensive piece of phone equipment can do. It offers all the features like Call Forwarding, Call Return, Conference Calling, music-on-hold, and so on. And I don't have to worry about it becoming obsolete."

Fact is, many times Centrex services can cost less than traditional phone lines, because you often don't need to order as many lines in the first place. Also, since all your lines are bridged together at the network level, you can buzz someone down the hall, using the same intercom-type function found in a typical PBX. Even better, if you have offices all over town, all using the Centrex services, you can buzz anyone on the system by punching only three or four keys. That means you can call someone clear across town the same as you would if they were two offices down the hall.

Centrex sales are booming. For example, look at Pacific Bell, which in 1996 announced reaching a milestone of 1.5 million lines. It introduced Centrex services in 1961, when sales were luke warm, at best. "It took us 32 years to reach the one million mark, but only three years to reach 1.5 million," notes Jim Murphy, Pac Bell's Centrex product director. "It's on a fourteen percent growth rate, which is quite respectable, to say the least."

Got the Need for Speed?
ISDN, T1, T3 and Beyond

"I've got the need for speed!" Remember that Tom Cruise line from *Top Gun*? Increasingly, today's business people are saying the same thing when it comes to Internet access. Regular phone lines and 28.8 modems just aren't fast enough for speed-hungry, busy business people.

Scott Williford, vice president of E.K. Williford & Associates, an Atlanta area telecommunications consultancy, decided to take the plunge. "I spend too much time on the Internet and it takes forever for page after slow page to materialize on my screen. I have to do something to speed things up. ISDN is my answer."

ISDN (Integrated Services Digital Network) sales are booming. BellSouth reported having more than 61,000 ISDN lines in service at the end of 1996. While minuscule in comparison to the more than 22 million total phone lines BellSouth operates, it's still more than twice the 1995 number of 29,000 ISDN lines.

Why is ISDN suddenly becoming so popular? Well, first of all, ISDN is simply a high-speed, digital, high-capacity phone line. It allows you to split the line into several uses. You can fax, log onto the Internet, check e-mail and have a conversation—all at the same time, on the same line. And the price is not significantly more than a regular single line or two. What a bargain. Digital allows for better use of the line for data-intensive communications like online surfing, video conferencing, data sharing, file transferring, and connecting to the office computer system from home.

ISDN is available for home or the office. How fast can it go? According to Forrester Research, downloading a two megabyte video clip takes:

- ❏ 18.5 minutes using a 14.4 modem, or
- ❏ 9.3 minutes on a 28.8 modem, or
- ❏ 2.1 minutes using ISDN.

That's why it's so popular. But even faster is T1, which would send that video clip in 10.7 seconds, or T3, which would send it in 0.4 seconds. Think about how far we've come. From 18 minutes to a half-second for the same amount of data. That's the stark reality of the disparity between services available today.

While ISDN is basically a no-brainer for most businesses, whether to use T1 or T3 is a more complicated decision. They don't make sense for most very small businesses until it has many dedicated phone lines. One T1 connection, using multiplexing technology and one pair of wires, can take the place of 24 dedicated lines, yet costs only a fraction of what 24 separate lines would cost. Talk with your local or long-distance company customer rep for an evaluation of your needs. If it makes sense, it can save you money and make your operation much more efficient.

What Do You Do When the Phones Go Out?

Okay, it happens to every business. You pick up the phone one day and hear nothing. In disbelief you hang up and try again. You try all your lines. Then you get that sinking feeling. You're dead in the water without phones. Most businesses can't function without phones. This happens to me every once in a while, and when it does, I lose critical links to the outside world—faxes, e-mail, Internet access and, of course, regular phone calls.

First, find a working phone, whether it be a neighbor's, your cellphone or even a payphone down the street. Report the problem. Determine if it's *your* phone or an area problem—some construction jockey on a backhoe down the street making spaghetti out of your underground phone lines.

Make sure you tell the service people that this is your business line and it's critical that the service be restored as soon as possible. Ask to be put on an expedited priority list. That's when you hear those frightening words, "We'll have the service back on by seven tomorrow night." *Yikes*! You've got to be kidding, but that's typical, so brace yourself. Service is often back up before then, but they want to cover themselves at the expense of your blood pressure.

Next, figure out what phone works. Sometimes, if you are lucky, you might have one or two lines on a different circuit that are still working. If not, consider your home phone. Ask the service operator to use emergency Call Forwarding and have them forward all calls coming to the dead phone to your home number. It's a bumpy ride, but at least you can still have a partial link to the world until the problem is corrected.

Cut Hackers Off at the Knees

DISA stands for Direct Inward System Access, and many companies keep DISA active on their phone lines around the clock. They do this so they can call in to their offices on their toll-free 800 lines to get messages from voice mail, to send messages, or to get an outbound line to make long-distance calls from wherever they are, which are then charged to their company. Only problem is, hackers have figured out how to do the same thing. Once they break your code, they can sell it on the black market, and before you know it, they've rung up tens of thousands of dollars in phone bills over a weekend. And phone companies hold customers fully responsible for the bill.

Small businesses are increasingly targeted by hackers because larger companies are catching on and making access more difficult. And, just like a thief will ignore a home with a security system in favor of the home next door without such protection, these hackers also look for the easy prey, the low-hanging fruit. Today, that's small business.

So turn off your DISA when you don't need it and keep alert for the telltale signs. If your phone bills show multiple attempts at your 800 lines in the middle of the night, or if your phone system logs multiple denials of attempts with incorrect passwords, that's a definite red flag that trouble might be lurking around the corner. Call your phone company and report suspicious activity immediately. In fact, it's a good idea to call them anyway and get their advice, and implement it as a preemptive precaution.

Area Code Shortage

Phone lines, fax lines, modem lines, cellular phones, pagers, and all the other high-tech communications tools are using up all the possible number combinations under the existing area code numbering scheme. This means that to increase the universe of numbers to dole out, we need to add new area codes. Region by region, new area codes are being rolled out. In 1997 alone, some 37 new codes were added. This creates confusion and the expense of printing new business cards and stationery, but there is no choice. If you've already experienced a new area code rollout in your area, you know what I am talking about. If not, it's only a matter of time.

To find the latest area codes, go to Bellcore's Web site at *www.bellcore.com.* Bellcore administers the North American Numbering Plan (NANP), assigning new codes as necessary. For an up-to-date area code map, try Aegis Publishing's Web site at *www.aegisbooks.com.*

One Number for all Your Locations

If you have locations all over town, you probably have separate phone numbers and let the customer determine which location is closer. Whether you have a dozen pizza delivery services or a half-dozen video rental stores around town, you can make it easier on your customers. Phone companies offer a service that allows all customers to dial one number and, based on their location, the call is forwarded to the closest shop. Some of the largest pizza delivery chains do this. It's not very expensive; even the smallest services can do this, but they don't. Why not? Most don't know this service even exists.

Follow Me, or One-Number Services

Is your business card beginning to look like a Rolodex? Increasingly, business people list many contact numbers, including office number, home number, pager, cellphone, fax, e-mail address, answering service, and so on. Think I'm exaggerating? Pull out your stack of contacts and take a gander. It's getting ridiculous. Not only is it unattractive, but it's also inefficient, and can even cost you business.

The average customer is just not going to work that hard to reach you. She will try the first number, maybe a second, but if she can't reach you, the next number she calls is that of your competitor. Make it as easy as possible for customers to reach you and to work with you. Take away all the impediments to doing business. Don't put the onus on them, because you will lose. And you will never know how much you've lost because these lost customers never got through or left a message in the first place.

New Follow Me or One-Number services use the power of the local, long-distance and cellular telephone companies' networks to deliver the call to you wherever you go. AT&T 500 numbers and MCI Directline are the two most widely-used services, but many other long-distance and local phone companies offer this service.

This is how they work: You arrange for one of these Follow Me numbers or services from your local, long-distance or cellular phone company. They are basically *smart* Call Forwarding services. You get one number that you can give out, on your business cards and advertisements. You program the number to ring in a pre-set pattern. For example, if a fax transmission comes in, the network recognizes it as such and routes the call to your fax machine, or to a fax mail box, for later retrieval. If it's a voice call, you can program it to ring your office phone first. Then, if you don't answer, it will reroute the call to your cellphone, then on to your home office, then, if all else fails, on to your pager or Voice Mail, or wherever you decide.

During the time it takes to route and reroute the call, a recorded message is typically heard by the caller, stating that it is trying to locate you. While callers don't always like to wait, they do realize that it's neat to have technology do the searching rather than having to track you down themselves. This not only cleans up your business card, but it also increases chances that customers will find you, which makes it easier for them to do business with you, and keeps you from missing any new opportunities.

Plumber Jack Aston is always out of the office, and frequently has his hands full of... well, let's leave it at that. He relies on these Follow Me services to make sure customers reach him. Since someone is not always in the office to answer the phone, this assures him that customers can reach him when they have an urgent call. As Aston says, "A clogged drain waits for no man."

If a call comes in when he is in the office, he answers it as usual. But when he leaves, the phone is programmed to track him down. "I used to lose business when frantic customers would call with an emergency and all they got was my answering machine," says Aston. "But now I am so busy with new work, there are days I have to turn away emergency work. It sure beats the alternative."

It's great for family emergencies, too. Nancy Casslebaum is a real estate agent. She is always out of the office showing homes and meeting with buyers and sellers, and she was losing business because of this. Then she started using a Follow Me service, and now all customer calls find her. More important, her family can reach her instantly as well.

"I was out showing property when I got an emergency call on my cellphone," she says. "It was the school saying my child had fallen on the playground and was hurt. I was able to be there within minutes to take care of her. The service automatically checked my office, then my home office, then my cellphone, in order to find me. That's how I programmed it. Thanks to this service, I was able to be there for my baby instead of having her wait for an hour or more, which is what would have happened in the old days, all of three months ago, before I started using this service."

Whether 500 numbers, 700 numbers or 800 numbers, these Follow Me numbers are available from many local, long-distance and cellular phone companies. They can be a real lifesaver by making it easier for the customer to find you and do business with you.

Shushing, E-mailing and Hot Tubbing

"Mountaintop Office Keeps Skiers in Touch" blared a *USA Today* front-page story on Friday, February 21, 1997. It talked about the new Sprint Communications Center, touted as a first-of-its-kind mountaintop business center, located in Vail, Colorado. While this might be the first, it's instant popularity guarantees that it will be the first of many.

This goes back to what we were talking about earlier. Many business people are finally able to take vacations and get away, thanks to being able to keep in touch. While this might defeat the purpose of getting away for many, the fact is that loads of entrepreneurs are hitting the slopes, the links, the beach, even their favorite fishin' hole, precisely because these communications tools enable them stay in touch. Without them, these folks would stay tied to their offices taking care of business. This definitely improves the quality of life for many folks and their families.

The article talked about investors tracking the rise or fall of their portfolios, e-mailing their brokers to execute transactions, or joining conference calls with clients worldwide. Sounds nuts, but that's where we are today. And to stay on top of your golf game... well, these are the new rules being written as we speak. These plugged-in getaways are merely a change of scenery, as opposed to the completely unplugged retreat, which would serve better for revitalizing the soul. But for many, these getaways are positive perks, enabled by technology.

Voice Mail:
Can't Live with It; Can't Live Without It

Customers say the only thing they hate more than getting your voice mail is when you don't have it, and they get nothing but endless ringing. Yes, voice mail is the butt of jokes and has become the technology everybody loves to hate, and it's easy to see why. When people call, they want to talk with someone, live. So they are naturally put off by not connecting. However, if they can't reach someone live, they'd prefer to leave a message and put the ball in someone else's court, rather than have to keep the call on their list of things to do.

Here are a few eye-opening comments from a typical customer who uses voice mail himself at work, and is frustrated when others don't reciprocate. See if you can pick up on his anguish.

"There's nothing more frustrating and aggravating than when I call a business after hours and they don't have voice mail, or even an answering machine," says Barry Lawson, a typical customer. "When I call my dentist to cancel an appointment, or my mechanic to ask when they open in the morning, I get nothing. No answering machine. Nothing. At least my accountant has an outgoing-only message letting me know he's closed. Big deal. As painful as it is to change, I am now looking for a new dentist and a new mechanic."

"The problem is, I'm too busy to play these games," continues Lawson, "I'm used to leaving a voice mail message nine out of 10 places I call. If they aren't there, or can't take the call, I can still leave a message and can still get things done. Projects move ahead, and messages get delivered, even if we don't talk real-time for weeks at a time. Since I'm used to that kind of connectivity at work, I have very little patience for the old-fashioned ways of not being in touch and not being reachable. If they make it difficult to do business, I go somewhere else."

It is that simple. This is what I've heard countless times from business customers and consumers. The bar is rising. The expectation level is rising. Customer demands and expectations are rising. Those businesses that don't rise to the challenge are bound to lose business.

Breaking Out of Voice Mail Jail

Set up and used right, voice mail is one of those great equalizers that can make your small business look big. Even if you don't care about looking big, voice mail can improve customer service, making them happy to keep doing business with you. It lets you selectively save or delete individual messages, customize different outbound messages, copy and forward messages to others in the company, send a message to a distribution list of mailbox users, and eliminate telephone tag—24 hours a day. It also saves time and money. The average voice mail message lasts less than a minute, as compared with more than three minutes for the average phone call. Add it up over all the calls made or received in a day, for each person in the organization.

However, don't be fooled. It's easy, but it takes some work to do it right. The mere use of a technology like voice mail is no guarantee of success and customer satisfaction, either. You've got to use it right. If you set things up badly, you can do more harm than good. Many businesses, large and small, shoot themselves in the foot by installing the latest technology willy-nilly, without concern for the customer's experience with it. Somehow, too many people have the idea that, by just writing a check and installing these systems, all their problems will be solved and the technology will automatically know how to interact with their customers.

The CEO of one of the largest banks in the country, in a highly publicized move, yanked out his company-wide voice mail system, which cost millions to install, after calling into the bank one day and hearing and experiencing what his customers hear and experience. Since then, the bank has gone through an evaluation process and reinstalled voice mail. This time, however, it works smoothly, giving customers what they want, how they want it.

Voice Mail Tips

When setting up or using voice mail keep in mind the following points:

❒ Customers frequently complain about getting trapped in voice mail with nowhere to go. Always program an escape hatch into your voice mail or auto attendant. Allow the caller to press "0" to be connected to a live operator.

❒ Voice mail is best when messages are kept brief and to the point. Voice mail is not good for long, detailed messages, since it requires the listener to stop and replay to jot down the whole message. Look to faxes or e-mail for that level of detail.

❒ In contrast to text messages, voice mail can convey emotions with your tone of voice. You can hear whether there is urgency, playfulness, humor or anger.

❒ However, voice mail is more urgent, so use it for that feature. Generally, "The phone is a more urgent means of communication than e-mail," says Elizabeth Powell, who teaches management communication at the University of Virginia's Darden Graduate School of Business.

❒ Don't hide behind voice mail. Be accessible to customers, and return calls as soon as possible.

❒ Check mail regularly. It can be a valuable tool, or a six gun pointed at your big toe, depending how you use it.

Toll Free and Vanity 800 Numbers

800 numbers have been around since 1967. Introduced by AT&T, they have grown in popularity in recent years. Now they are available from all long-distance and local phone companies. Thanks to 800 portability, initiated in 1993, you can now keep your 800 number even if you switch phone companies. Previously, you had to stay with your carrier to keep the same number. If you switched, you'd have to give up your number, because each carrier was assigned its own pool of numbers. Changing numbers was costly, since so much was spent advertising and promoting the number. It was so costly that many businesses stayed with the carrier even though they wanted to switch. Toll free numbers are now administered by Database Services Management, Inc., but you, the company that uses the 800 number, own the 800 number (as long as you pay your bill).

Prices have dropped so low that every business should consider having a toll-free number. It can cost as little as a few dollars per month plus a competitive per-minute rate, and you no longer have to have a dedicated line. The calls on the 800 number can "piggyback" onto your local phone line. This is called "switched services." Of course, don't ignore the benefits of dedicated lines if your business is an intensive user of 800 services. Either option gives you the power to have calls forwarded to other offices, or even to your home or your technician's home on weekends, so you remain in total control. What a system!

Maybe you have dialed one of thousands of vanity numbers, such as 1-800-FLOWERS, 1-800-HILTONS or 1-800-CAR-RENT. Large companies have been leveraging vanity 800 numbers for years. It's one of the most powerful marketing tools at your disposal. Some companies use it as a pillar of their marketing campaign. Others, as in 1-800-FLOWERS, use it as the front door to their virtual storefronts.

Customers love them because they don't have to remember long, meaningless numbers. Or search for a pen while driving after hearing an ad on the radio. They're easy to remember. There's that rule again about *making it easier for the customer to do business with you*. Removing the impediments.

Many businesses have found their numbers are as good as gold—a valuable business asset. There are a few downsides, however. You are responsible for all charges. Let's say a business from the other side of the country has a 800 number similar to yours; only one of the numbers is different. Then let's say it places a big ad in numerous papers to promote something, but someone makes a typo and the number that is published is yours. *Yikes!* You can get dozens, hundreds, even thousands of calls, tying up your lines and your people, and to add insult to injury, *you* are responsible for the cost of all those calls. Not fair, you might say. Darn right it's not fair. But that's life. Part of the cost of doing business.

Even so, the use of 800 numbers is continuing its meteoric rise. They are valuable enough to take that risk. They are growing so rapidly that not long ago we effectively ran out of 800 numbers. If you've tried to get an 800 number lately, you've no doubt noticed there are none left. You now have to get an 888 number, which works the same, but it's wreaking havoc with customers and companies alike. Often customers dial 800 instead of 888 and don't understand why they didn't reach the intended party. Customers are frustrated. So are the owners of the 888 numbers who missed the call. So are the owners of the 800 number who didn't want the call, but got it anyway, plus the bill.

The *Wall Street Journal* recently ran a piece on another pothole on the toll-free highway. What happens when a company spends hundreds of thousands—or millions—of dollars to create a level of recognition for its 800 number, then the same number, but with the 888 prefix, is given to a competitor? For instance, if a lesser-known flower shop could get its hands on 1-888-FLOWERS, it could live off the scraps of the original's marketing efforts. Should the 888 version be offered to the owner of the original 800 version on a first-right-of-refusal basis?

And what about the bandits who buy numbers in bulk and then charge confiscatory rates to sell similar numbers to companies that own the originals. To protect their interests, the victimized companies often spend the money, but is it fair? This issue is still being debated, but until it's resolved, the 888 vanity numbers in question have been taken out of the pool. With all this said, there are still many valid reasons why you should not be without a toll-free number. After all, this must be a small price to pay judging by their continued popularity. In fact, we are running out of 888 numbers now, too. Expect 877 to be out in April 1998, and 866 to follow soon thereafter.

A study released a couple years ago by the Technical Assistance Research Program looked at the value of 800 numbers, and it was clear that every business that deals with consumers would benefit by having a toll-free number. If your competitors have one, and you don't, the choice of whom to call is clear to your customers.

Many customers won't even place the call if they have to spend their dime. We've been conditioned that way over the years. More interesting, however, was the finding that 86% of consumers believe that toll-free numbers on packages connote quality products. Another very important advantage. "We get immediate feedback on our products," says a Starkist Foods spokesperson in another *Wall Street Journal* article.

If You Always Wanted to be a Phone Company

Smart businesses are realizing there is a big opportunity in offering telephone services to their customers on a resale basis. If you have a large customer base, and are always looking for ways to offer more value and more services to them, consider reselling telephone services.

Forrester Research, while studying how many larger businesses use telecom strategically, found that companies are becoming carriers themselves. Companies such as Hertz, General Electric,

Delta Airlines and many others are making telecom services available to their customers, and even to non-customers, as either a profit center or as an entirely separate business unit. General Electric started GE Exchange, which is one of the nation's largest resellers of telephone service. Delta Airlines has taken the same route by making phone cards, inbound 800 service, and even outbound long-distance service available to any business or consumer.

The key here is that these companies already use and manage these telephone services for their own operations. Allowing additional users on board increases the traffic they generate with their phone company, which allows them to negotiate even lower rates. Additionally, they are able to make a nice profit on the new customers, while at the same time offering these customers a discount off what they were paying before. From the customer perspective, it can be a good deal, although the customer service provided by the resale companies is rarely as good as that provided by the phone companies themselves. However, from the reseller's perspective, it's a great additional service to offer customers, not to mention a potentially lucrative a profit center.

You don't have to be a large company to use this idea. Many smaller business are doing this successfully. But instead of reselling the services they already contract for, they simply sign up with a carrier to become a reseller at the outset. This allows the small business to get a special reseller discount so it can mark-up the service a bit to make a profit, at the same time offering its own customers a value-added service.

Lilly Walters of Walters Speaker Services, one of the leading speakers bureaus in the country, has figured out this profitable secret and weaves it seamlessly into her agency's service offerings. This is a value-added service that Walters offers to her huge base of clients and contacts. By the way, this is a book on communications, and if public speaking is in your past, present or future, you've got to get Dottie and Lilly Walters' books, *Speak and Grow Rich* and *Secrets of Successful Speakers*. They've helped me immeasurably to understand the business of speaking, and I heartily recommend these volumes as required reading.

Billing Services Let You
Track and Manage Calls and Expenses

Many businesses have the need to track expenses and bill them back to clients for reimbursement. Telephone expense reimbursements are typically included in such a charge to the client. Enhanced billing features from today's local and long-distance companies can make that job much easier. Custom billing solutions are becoming more prevalent with each passing year, allowing you to customize your billing according to the way you work, tailoring it to the needs of your firm. You can even get your billing on a computer disk so you can analyze and manage the data any way you see fit. This allows you to create separate bills to send to each client based on any scenario you select.

Some of the most popular billing features include:

- Bundling of all your locations into one bill.
- Breaking calls out by location, employee, project, client, etc.
- Separate bills generated for each client for reimbursement.

These are very powerful tools for measuring, cost control, and to make sure you are using telecom services efficiently. Use them. You can order Call Accounting services from your phone companies, or you can purchase a hardware/software add-on for your phone system.

The phone company version is more cost effective and more accurate. However, it doesn't measure each individual call. The commercial hardware/software versions are less accurate but measure each call. For example, the long-distance company's Call Accounting service measures long-distance calls only, not your local calls. Likewise, your local phone company will track only local calls.

The phone company call accounting is accomplished by tracking the outbound caller, where each caller is assigned his own two- or three-digit code, which he must enter before each long-distance call is completed. Hardware/software call accounting systems, on the other hand, measure each call by station, not by caller. These systems measure every call made from each phone, no matter who made the call.

Both ways have advantages and disadvantages. It's up to each individual customer to decide which is best for his or her firm's needs.

Audio/Video/Document Conferencing: As Good as Being There... Almost

Gathering folks together for meetings from near and far is getting tougher all the time. Forget far! Even from *near* it's darned near impossible, given our frantic pace of business. That's why conferencing is exploding in popularity.

Brain power from across the hall and across the globe can gather in minutes, just by picking up the phone or logging in on the desktop or notebook computer, no matter where everyone is actually located. People call into conference calls from their offices, homes, hotels, car phones, airport pay phones, or wherever they happen to be. That's the simplicity and power that makes this such an effective tool.

Conferencing technologies have evolved over the last few years. There are Audio Conference calls, which are by far the most common and the easiest to set up. Video Conferencing and Document Conferencing are also growing in popularity, and will likely become as widespread as faxing within a few years.

Audio Conferencing:
You Should Hear What You are Missing

Audio Conferencing comes in many flavors. Local phone companies offer three-way-calling type services as a network-level service like Call Waiting or Call Forwarding. For a few dollars a month, you can set up a simple conference call between you and two other people by using your telephone keypad, dialing the assigned code, and then dialing the phone numbers of the other parties.

Dale Keiting loves three-way-calling. "At the touch of a few buttons, I can conference in a third person when a conversation needs a third opinion or when we need to run something by somebody else," she says. Beyond the monthly charge, there are no additional charges for the service. Calls are billed at their normal rate for local or long-distance, depending on the call.

More people to link up? There are other services available from long-distance and local phone companies that allow you to hook up a virtually limitless number of people on a huge conference call. Typically, the call is set up in advance with the phone company of choice and handled by an operator, or coordinator. An 800 call-in number is disseminated to the participants, who all call in at a predetermined time. One by one, as they call in, they are patched into the call with the others by the operator at the phone company.

There is usually a per-call charge and a per-minute charge for each participant, which covers the use of the toll-free 800 call-in number. You can avoid this charge by having each person call into a regular number so they pay for the long-distance call. This is usually determined by the relationship among the participants. For instance, you shouldn't expect customers to pay for a call to hear a sales pitch, or reporters to pay to hear a press announcement. Conference-calling service bureaus have recently sprung up whose business is to orchestrate such calls. They also charge per connection and per minute, similar to phone companies.

I've participated in hundreds of these calls over the years, some with as few as three or four on a call. Others, like big press conferences or analysts' briefings, have had hundreds of people on the line. When juggling this many, the participants typically are in a listen-only mode, at least initially, such as when a presentation is given. After the presentation is complete, the lines are opened two ways for questions and answers, and each party with a question can push a key on the phone to establish a position in the queue, and when it's his or her turn, the question is asked for all to hear, along with the answer.

These big conference calls were once the tool of only the largest companies. Now that the service is available from your phone company, small businesses are tapping its power and getting more done, more efficiently.

Video conferencing is the next step, and it will be covered in Chapter 5.

Prepaid Phone Cards: All the Rage

All of a sudden, prepaid telephone cards, also known as telecards, are popping up everywhere. TV networks and movie studios are giving away or selling the cards as promotional items, imprinted with pictures of hit shows and stars. They're being sold in vending machines at airports, at convenience stores, and in office supply stores. Like imprinted coffee mugs and other advertising specialties, they are used as marketing giveaways, often included along with other products. They're popping up all over town and all over the country. Small businesses are starting to tap into their marketing power.

Prepaid phone cards have been popular in Europe since the '70s, but didn't make it to U.S. shores until the early '90s. Since then, they've exploded. In 1996, they were a $1 billion part of the industry and growing at a whopping 25% per year. Some analysts predict a $2.5 billion market by the year 2000. What? You don't use prepaid phone cards in your business? Then you're missing a terrific marketing and business tool. Innovative businesses are using this new tool to increase profits, generate business, control costs and build goodwill.

This is how the cards work. They look like credit cards, or long-distance calling cards, but they don't work the same way. Instead of billing you at the end of the month for the calls you made, you pay for phone time up-front, prepaying for a certain amount of usage (measured in units or minutes). The holder can use the card at any phone to place long-distance calls until the prepaid amount is used up. When the time is depleted, the cardholder can usually purchase more time to recharge the card, by calling a customer-service number and paying over the phone with a credit card, or they can simply buy another card and scrap the old one.

How are businesses using these prepaid cards to make money? Here are a few ways:

❒ *Sell the card:* Many businesses sell the cards to their customers. They are very popular at retail establishments, convenience stores, newsstands and travel-related businesses such as hotels, motels, car rentals, restaurants, gift shops, souvenir shops, gas stations, parking lots, and taxi stands—any place that has a good traffic flow of customers. They are especially useful to customers who travel, or who deal in cash, out of preference or necessity. The cards are a high-profit, low-maintenance product. The retail display can take up as little or as much space as you choose.

❒ *Give to traveling employees:* Giving out a regular long-distance calling card is like giving an employee a blank check. He can charge as much as he wants. Abuse is common. Prepaid cards automatically limit the amount an employee can call, so he is less likely to abuse the privilege, using the card primarily for business purposes.

❒ *Give away to customers:* Customers love giveaways. Businesses are always looking for valuable premiums to give away in order to win favor with their customers. Because everyone uses long-distance, everyone will love this one. Forget the calendars, pens and magnets. Customers will love receiving free-long distance and they will remember you—especially if the card has your name and logo imprinted on it.

❒ *Incentives:* These make great prizes for employee or customer contests.

❒ *Holiday gifts:* At holiday time, employees and customers appreciate them more than the traditional turkeys, or the baskets of smoked-cheese-pepperoni-popcorn-crackers. And they're not fattening.

❒ *Prevent toll fraud/theft:* Toll fraud is a growing problem. Phone thieves steal telephone calling card numbers and ring up huge phone bills over a month's time before the customer gets her bill and realizes what has happened. With prepaid cards, on the other hand, you can lose only up to the face amount on the card itself—a relatively smaller amount.

❒ *Joint marketing ventures:* Strike up a marketing deal with another company whose customers fit the same profile as yours. Insert prepaid phone cards with your company name and offer inside their products, and they can do likewise with your products.

These are only a few of the innovative ways companies are using these tools to build their business, make money and save money. I'll bet you can think of many more applications for your particular business.

You can purchase prepaid phone cards from many suppliers these days. However, I'd advise going with a well-known long-distance carrier rather than a smaller operation. First of all, people like getting a brand name they recognize rather than a no-name product. There is more perceived value. Also, problems with of some smaller firms have been reported, where they couldn't deliver the service that was initially agreed upon.

Prepaid phone cards are much more than long-distance calling cards. They are powerful marketing tools. Don't let this one pass you by. It's a terrific and inexpensive way to build your business and control costs, and your competition might not be using phone cards yet!

900 Pay-Per-Call Lines: Going Legit and Going Big Time

For many years 900 numbers, 976 numbers and the entire pay-per-call business was full of mostly adult chat lines, psychic hotlines, and an assortment of shady programs of dubious value. So what's new, you might ask? Well, there still are plenty of those types of services. In fact, much can be learned from those marketers. After all, many of them do make fortunes. But something else is happening: The 900 pay-per-call industry is maturing and going mainstream.

Companies such as Microsoft, CompUSA and thousands of others are offering support and information lines, jumping on the pay-per-call bandwagon with enthusiasm. So are companies like the *Wall Street Journal*, NBC, *USA Today*, and assorted other news and entertainment companies. All in all, there are thousands of large and small businesses using pay-per-call services to offer information or advice, often turning it into a business in-and-of itself, or at least a separate profit center.

Fitness Club Uses 900 Number for Membership Upgrades

Bally Total Fitness clubs have been using a 900 number since 1995. Members dial 900-370-CARD in order to upgrade their current membership card to an enhanced membership card, for a flat charge of $10 per call, which is included on their next telephone bill.

This service is offered strictly to existing members, and approximately 1,500 to 3,000 of them call in each month to upgrade their membership. The line is completely automated, requiring no live attendants to complete the transaction. In fact, one of the reasons behind initiating the line was because the Membership Services department was swamped with calls, making it difficult for members to get through to upgrade their membership status. The line provides a valuable service to Bally's members by making it very easy to upgrade membership at any time. And the method of payment couldn't be easier.

Big East Briefs Hotline

Greg Shemitz, based in Middle Village, New York, nearly doubled his income after launching his *Big East Briefs* Hotline (900-860-3400, 95¢ per minute) to complement his *Big East Briefs* newsletter. The newsletter, now in its ninth season, is published 16 times a year ($42 annual subscription) and covers Big East basketball, including in-depth recruiting reports, league news, behind-the-scenes recruiting analysis and interviews with Big East recruiters and high school coaches with promising prospects.

Shemitz is serving a niche of nearly 2,000 subscribers, hard-core Big East fans who also appreciate getting the most up-to-date information possible via the 900-number hotline. Shemitz is using the hotline to augment the information in the newsletter with fast-breaking news about recruiting — providing better service to his appreciative customers.

The peak calling periods coincide with the spring and fall signing periods. The hotline will get an average of 150 to 200 calls per day, with the content updated daily. During non-peak periods the rest of the year, the hotline generates about 100 calls per update, which is twice a week.

Shemitz updates the line himself, reporting each update like a brief news item. The line has been operational since January 1994.

Although he doesn't have any hard data to back it up, Shemitz believes that nearly all his callers are loyal subscribers, many of whom have memorized the 900 number. When asked whether there was a measurable spike in calls after mailing out the newsletter, Shemitz indicated that there was only a small increase. This is a good example of a line that generates substantial repeat calls despite the frequency of advertising.

For more information about setting up a 900-number service, read *900 Know-How* (Aegis, 1996, $19.95) by Robert Mastin. An excellent start-up guide.

Phone Companies Help You Keep Up to Date

Perpetual learning is the only viable way to keep up with all the changes in technology and , thus, keep your edge. Fortunately, the phone companies want to be your friend by helping you with your business, so they offer a wealth of educational materials and programs. They present a regular slate of seminars educating customers on their services. They have home pages on the Internet with loads of small-business resources. They provide books and other information to help customers understand the changes in the industry and to help customers save and make money with their services. You'd be wise to take them up on their standing offers of help.

Chapter 5
Taking Advantage of
Cutting-Edge Technology

Advances in telecommunications technology have levelled the playing field. The smallest businesses can give the appearance of being as big as their largest rivals. Armed with the right combination of equipment and services, any business can present itself to the world as a sophisticated, technically savvy organization that is impossible to differentiate from a competitor that might be hundreds of times larger.

In the last chapter we discussed the various services offered by the phone companies. Many of the services covered in this chapter may eventually be offered by the phone companies, but this chapter focuses more on what some of the new equipment can do for you. For now, most of this equipment would be purchased and installed in your facility. Some of the products are PC-based and relatively inexpensive. Keep in mind that the technology is advancing rapidly, while at the same time the cost of buying the technology continually falls.

The same market- and technology-driven trends that have resulted in huge increases in computing power, while costs continue to plummet, will also benefit the telephone.

Computer-Telephone Integration
Means Smart Phones

You may have probably heard the terms *computer-telephone integration* and *computer telephony*. What do they really mean? Both terms mean the same thing: smart telephones. Computers are digital. Telephones are becoming digital. Sophisticated telephones and telecom systems use computer chips or even dedicated computers. Computers talk to each other over phone lines. There is a convergence of computer and telephone technologies. The advances in computers have spurred some very smart telephones and phone systems.

This chapter will cover some of the new technologies such as Voice Recognition, Interactive Voice Response, Audiotex, Fax-on-Demand, Video Conferencing, and others. These exciting new capabilities are the end result of computer-telephone integration. In the not-too-distant future a computer will be an integral part of your telephone, or vice versa. Your contact list and phone numbers will be stored on your computer, which will also keep a record of all communications with your customers, vendors, friends and associates. Your telephone/computer will be a multi-featured communications system that will be able to handle voice mail, fax broadcasting, e-mail, and just about any other new technology feature you can conceive of. It will also be programmable, so you can configure the system to suit your specific needs.

This might sound futuristic, but the technology is already here. Early versions of such systems are already in the marketplace. Bugs are being worked out and the functionality is improving. There are stand-alone systems that look like supercharged answering machines. Then there are the fully programmable PC-based systems that offer superb flexibility. And the phone companies are offering more and more network-based services based on these technologies. The management of communications is getting much easier.

Fax-on-Demand Offers
24-Hour Customer Service

With the growing popularity of e-mail, the Internet and assorted other new technologies, many people question if this spells the end for traditional faxing. In reality, faxing has never been hotter, thanks to all the enhanced fax services like fax-on-demand and fax broadcast.

Fax-on-demand (FOD) is a good example of how computer-telephone integration is empowering businesses of all sizes. A fax-on-demand system can be either proprietary system or PC-based. Or such services can be purchased from a service provider.

FOD is simple: Documents are stored on a computer's hard drive, and each is assigned a number, which is listed on a menu of selections. The menu itself is often the first document choice available. The caller selects the document, which is faxed to his or her fax machine.

The actual dialing can be one- or two-legged. For a one-legged call, where the caller pays for the long-distance phone call (or if a pay-per-call 900 number is used), the caller must call from the handset on her fax machine, pressing the *start* button when instructed to do so. On a two-legged call, the caller is asked to input the fax number, via the keypad, where she wishes to receive the fax, and the system calls that number back and transmits the document.

FOD saves a lot of time and money. It's completely automated, freeing your customer-service representatives from dealing with repetitive requests for information, allowing them to tackle the more challenging situations that require human attention. It saves paper, and virtually any printed document can be stored in the system, such as catalogs, specification sheets, operating instructions, price lists, news releases, product announcements, locator maps, hiring policies, or any other information you want to communicate in printed form to a wide audience on a regular basis. And it's available 24 hours a day, at the convenience of the caller.

Information Engineering is a small firm on the East coast with clients all over the country. "Our biggest problem was not being available for clients on the West coast who called in for standard, frequently-requested information. It wasn't brain surgery. It was standard information, instructions or schematics they were looking for, but we weren't able to get it to our clients who called us after hours. It really hindered our growth prospects. Once we started using fax-on-demand, all that changed. Now, our clients can call anytime, day or night, and get the frequently-requested printed material sent to them using our automated system. At first we used a service provider, then we set up our own dedicated computer." The bottom line: Since Information Engineering is no longer giving its West coast clients the silent treatment, business from that area has increased dramatically.

Surprisingly, even some of the largest companies, such as Microsoft, don't maintain a 24-hour live customer-service support line. Like most other users, I have often called after hours only to be greeted by a friendly voice telling me to call tomorrow. For more frequent questions however, Microsoft has developed a very extensive fax-on-demand system. You can get the answer to countless questions, and solutions to a wide range of common problems, by simply using the prompts and having documents faxed right to your fax machine, 24 hours a day.

Small businesses that don't offer 24-hour live customer service are also taking advantage of this same powerful tool, just like Microsoft, IBM, Toshiba and a whole host of other customer-intensive companies.

Cambridge Computers is a mail-order computer business. It mans customer-service lines during business hours only. From 8 p.m. until 8 a.m. the next morning, customers cannot reach a live customer-service representative. However, Cambridge has made extensive use of both fax-on-demand and its Internet site to provide a wealth of information to after-hours callers. "We found that more than half of the customers who call in for customer service or technical support after hours get their questions answered through our automated systems. The rest call us in the morning. But since we can track how many calls we get and how many don't call back in the morning, we figure we're doing a pretty good job. Our customers tell us we do, anyway."

Putting Old Computers to New Uses

Don't think that the only option is to go out and buy an expensive new fax server in order to deploy enhanced fax services. If you have an old 486—or even a 386—computer lying around collecting dust, this could do the trick. It should be able to handle the fax software with no problem. The issue is only one of reliability. The computer will be running for long periods of time unattended, so it needs to be fairly robust. And an uninterruptible power supply (UPS) will be good insurance against power failures and irregularities.

Today's Voice Mail: Paving the Way for Tomorrow's Messaging

If you hate dealing with voice mail, you'd better look for a good place to hide because Video Mail is on the way. You'll send messages by talking into your desktop video/phone setup, and receive messages the same way. Not every call will have a picture. You'll get a combination of voice-only and voice/video messages. But as video technology becomes cheaper, standardized and more widespread, it will become part of every pay phone, cellphone, home and office phone. Get used to the idea, because it's coming soon.

Managing Voice Messaging with Automated Attendants, ACD, IVR and Audiotex

When customers call in, how do you handle and distribute their calls? A receptionist used to handle the screening and distribution of calls, sending them to the intended party or taking a message if they were out. Today, AAs, (automated attendants), ACDs (automatic call distributors) and IVR (interactive voice response) systems are becoming increasingly user-friendly and popular, and are replacing receptionists—or at least augmenting them.

Think about what you hear when you call larger companies. AAs and ACDs will answer the phone when you call a busy reservations number, for example. A recording tells the caller, "All agents are busy with other callers. Please stay on the line and someone will be with you in the order you called." The ACD puts the call in queue and automatically sends it to an agent when one becomes available.

IVR and Audiotex allow your caller to find a particular party or department. They also allow you to make all sorts of information available to customers, who simply follow the recorded voice instructions and press the right keys on the telephone keypad. Thus, the call winds its way through a maze of preconfigured information responses until the caller gets the information she called for.

Stephanie Green operates an information-intensive service business. "Clients and prospects are calling in all the time for the same information," she says. "These services offer my business many benefits, including being available twenty-four hours a day, being much cheaper than having live personnel staff the phones, and having the ability to handle many calls at once, gracefully. That's something even our best receptionist struggled with."

Where to Get it

Voice Mail, AA, ACD, IVR and Audiotex are all computer-driven technologies. You can get them a variety of ways:

❐ You can buy a sophisticated stand-alone system from a telephone equipment vendor or a computer store.

❐ Special software can transform an existing PC in your office into a Voice Messaging system.

❐ The top-of-the-line digital answering machines often come equipped with voice mail features, and are available at many office supply retailers.

❐ Telecom service bureaus offer many of these messaging services, and can offer custom solutions based on your specific needs.

❐ You can order these services directly from your phone company, as a network service, so you don't have to purchase the equipment yourself. This way, you use the state-of-the-art technology from the phone company and let them worry about maintaining and upgrading the equipment.

These messaging technologies can be real customer service and productivity boosters, if done right. The best judges of how well it works are the users, whether they be employees or customers, at five- or 5,000-person offices. Ask them. Ask them to be honest, and take heed of their answers. You might not like what you hear, but hear it you must.

While these technologies can make money and keep customers happy, like any good double-edged sword, they can also be costly and harmful if used badly. A poorly set-up voice mail system is a productivity buster for employees. A bad system for customers will cost you business. Make sure you do it right, and remember to make an occasional call to your own voice mail system; it can be an eye-opener.

Tip: If callers are seeking help from a live person, limit the number of menu choices to two or three levels before reaching an operator. And make sure there actually is a live person at the end of the trail. I can't tell you how many customers push their way though a half-dozen levels to get to the person they want—only to be greeted by, "Hi. Sorry I'm away from my desk/on the other line/ out of the office/away on vacation/not taking calls. . . please leave a message." *AAAAAAArrrrrrrrrggggggghhhhhhh!*

Always give the caller the choice of hitting "0" to get a live operator instantly. This is one of the most important tips in this section. If a customer knows he is calling an automated system, he won't mind pressing "1" for this and "2" for that all day. But if he is calling to ask a question or talk to a person, he'll have a very short fuse. Callers are often so angry by the time they reach someone that the problem they called about is dwarfed by the frustration developed while winding their way through voice mail jail.

What's it Good for?

IVR and Audiotex can really help you make money. These systems can take orders, give out customer support, deliver sales or service information to customers, distribute company information and news to employees, gather customer information, provide account information, and so on. The possibilities are endless. Information of any kind can be delivered or collected.

Think of your business. What information are you repeatedly asked for by customers, employees and prospects? Here are just a few examples of how IVR and Audiotex systems are used:

❑ Banks provide 24-hour account information.

- ❐ Restaurants provide menu and specials-of-the-day information.
- ❐ Retail stores provide hours and directions.
- ❐ Doctors offices provide hours and emergency contact information.
- ❐ Movie theaters provide movie times and listings. Moviefone receives up to two million calls per week using IVR. It even sells advertising. Local theaters should take heed.
- ❐ Golf courses allow callers to reserve tee times.

Provide Automated 24-Hours-a-Day Customer Service

You can automate many of your frequent information requests and serve your customers 24 hours a day, seven days a week. It used to be that only larger companies could provide "24 x 7 x 365" customer support and service. Now even the smallest of businesses can do so. Customers are demanding this kind of access, and increasingly, large and small businesses are heeding the call and offering this benefit. It's a competitive advantage for now, but it will quickly become a core expectation.

Think you don't need 24-hour-a-day customer support? Think your customer—who has a simple but important question at 10 o'clock at night, after putting the kids to bed and finally getting the chance to sit down to use your product or service—is going to be happy when he can't reach you and get the simple answer to the question which is keeping him from using and enjoying your widget? Especially when your competitor advertises 24-hour customer support. Think again.

Order Taking Made Easy with IVR

Ben Arnold Company is a large distributor of wine and spirits in South Carolina. Before the system was automated, the salespeople phoned in their orders from the road, often recording the order on an answering machine if they couldn't get through to a person.

The problems with this procedure were rampant: The manual order-taking and data-entry process was prone to human errors; it took a lot of time; phone costs were high; there were not enough people to handle all the calls during peak hours; salespeople were spending too much time on the phone placing orders instead of selling product; and orders had to be phoned in only during normal working hours.

The company decided to install an IVR system that would automate the ordering process. The system supports both touch-tone telephones and handheld terminals for order entry with voice response.

Using the touch-tone keypad, salespeople could make inquiries into the computer's database about product availability or verify the customer's credit-worthiness by checking for overdue invoices. The order is then placed using the telephone keypad, responding to pre-recorded voice prompts and instructions. The order is processed and verified instantly while the salesperson is still on the line, and the system will alert the caller if there are any errors in the order itself, or if any of the ordered items are out of stock.

For high-volume orders, salespeople were provided with pre-programmed handheld terminals that are capable of storing multiple orders spanning a full week. To transmit the orders, the salesperson calls into the system and follows the voice instructions to connect the terminal and transmit the data. This handheld terminal is helpful for taking orders as the salesperson walks around the store with the customer, building the customer's order on the fly.

This system has yielded many benefits for Ben Arnold Company. It has saved money by reducing telephone and order-entry costs. It has reduced errors and speeded up deliveries. Salespeople are seeing more customers and selling more product. And the customers are happy because they are getting better service at every turn.

Compliance with Government Regulations Easier with IVR

Crawford & Company, a risk-management company based in Atlanta, uses an IVR system to report its compliance with federal agency applicant tracking rules. According to Mary Neuman, a lead systems analyst at the company, the goal was to improve compliance with a "very simple system."

Federal agency reporting requires information about each position that is filled by the company, such as how many applicants were interviewed, their ethnicity and gender, how many were offered the position, and how many turned the offer down. Before the IVR system was installed, this was handled with paperwork, which was complicated, burdensome and time consuming.

The IVR system solved this problem. Now the hiring managers, located in all 50 states, simply call into the system and answer a series of pre-recorded questions. It couldn't be any easier. The data collected by the IVR system is exported to a Lotus spreadsheet program which automatically generates the required paperwork. According to Neuman, this new system makes it much easier to stay in full compliance with federal agency reporting requirements.

Automated Payroll Saves Time and Paperwork

ACTMEDIA is a major provider of in-store marketing, promotion and merchandising services to the retail industry. Headquartered in Norwalk, Connecticut, the company's employees are located in 35 field offices all over the U.S., and they spend a lot of time on the road visiting retail clients.

In order to simplify the collection and processing of payroll data, and to improve the timeliness and accuracy of reports to its clients, ACTMEDIA decided to install an IVR system from Periphonics Corporation (516-468-9000) that provides touch-tone payroll service to employees. The service allows employees to report information such as hours worked, mileage traveled and expenses incurred—through the use of the telephone keypad. To ensure accuracy, after the data is entered, the system repeats the information to the caller for confirmation.

"The automated service has been very convenient for our employees," says Don Grenier, senior vice president of information services. "It took them just a few days to learn how to use it, and now all of their payroll transactions are handled by the system. The service allows them to call in their information while they are on the road, and saves them the trouble of filling out various expense and payroll forms. And by speeding up the payroll process, we can ensure faster delivery of paychecks."

Newspaper Subscriptions With IVR

The *Milwaukee Journal Sentinel* wanted to improve customer service without hiring new employees. "In our industry, we strive to be as responsive to our subscribers as possible," says Gloria Najera, circulation consumer services director. "Our goal is to ensure that all service-related calls are answered within 20 seconds. Since staffing and payroll costs take up a large portion of our budget, we wanted to achieve that goal without increasing our overhead. After extensive research, we determined that the most efficient way to do that was to automate routine transactions."

The newspaper installed an IVR system that automates several functions that were previously handled by employees. The service allows subscribers to access account and billing information, renew subscriptions, stop and re-start delivery during vacations, pay for subscriptions with credit cards, and enter complaints. Because it's entirely automated, subscribers can use the system 24 hours a day and get right through with no delay. The system handles an average of 3,000 calls per month, about 15% of the newspaper's customer service call volume.

It's midnight and you just finished packing for a one-week vacation, and you're scheduled for a 4 a.m. flight the next morning. But you forgot to call the newspaper to suspend deliveries while you're away. No problem; dial the IVR system and take care of it right now, because you might forget to call tomorrow when you will be tied up doing the important stuff, like hitting golf balls.

Callers requiring more personalized attention can transfer to a live customer-service representative during regular business hours. "The IVR system handles most routine transactions, allowing our customer service staff to concentrate on those customers with more complex inquiries," says Najera. "Since installing the systems, we have seen our call abandonment rate decrease significantly. Our subscribers no longer receive busy signals or wait on hold when calling for service. We are able to contain our payroll costs and increase the efficiency of our call center staff, while improving the services available to our subscribers."

The service consists of two VPS/is 7500 IVR systems from Periphonics, with a capacity of 32 ports (lines). "We want to encourage our subscribers to use the automated service," says Najera. "The IVR system ensures that calls will be answered and completed quickly and accurately. The service is becoming increasingly popular with our subscribers. As call volumes grow, we expect to further enhance the service by adding additional applications and possibly expanding port capacity."

Automated Retirement Information

The Teachers' Retirement System (TRS) of the City of New York improved efficiency by installing an automated IVR system. The system, which provides 24-hour service to active and retired members, offers up-to-date information of interest to all members:

- ☐ The balance on existing loans.
- ☐ The current amount a member may borrow, and projected loan payments.
- ☐ The latest unit values for the variable annuity programs.
- ☐ A reliable way to order forms and publications.
- ☐ Answers to almost 200 commonly-asked questions.

The system also has speech recognition capabilities for members who call in on rotary phones. "Speech recognition is used as a menu navigation tool," says George Rose, a computer associate at TRS. "It is also used to select one of the many answers to frequently-asked questions by speaking up to three digits to choose the question. Callers get a quick, authoritative answer without ever having to speak to a representative." Topics range from becoming a member to service retirement plans to death benefits.

The system averages about 6,500 calls per month, and has peaked at 9,500 calls in a busy month. "If you were to consider the number of operators that would be needed to answer almost 10,000 phone calls in a month, the necessity and efficiency of the system becomes quite clear," says Rose.

IVR Simplifies Student Registration

St. John's University in New York uses an IVR system to serve its student population. It currently offers two helpful functions: disseminating grades and registering for classes. Nearly all of the University's 18,000 students commute to school from home, so the IVR system allows them to access their grades from their home telephone. When students call into the system, they must enter their social security number and PIN number. The computer first validates this data, then provides a menu selection from which they can choose to hear their grades, or register for classes for an upcoming semester.

The feedback from students using the system has been positive, and plans are underway to expand the system. TDD access for the hearing-impaired is planned, as well as credit card payment of tuition through touch-tone input. The IVR system will also be programmed to process financial aid applications.

Voice Mail as a Business

Many entrepreneurs, after seeing the value of new technologies, get so excited that instead of implementing it into their current businesses, they start a new business around the technology itself. Ken Leebow was a successful accountant until the technology bug bit him several years ago. "After seeing the potential voice mail had to change the way people communicate, I just knew I had to be part of it," he says.

So he pulled together the capital, invested in the latest voice mail computer system and started renting voice mail boxes to small businesses. It was one of the earliest voice mail service bureaus in booming suburban Atlanta. His company, Voice Information Processing, has grown over the years to offer pagers and other assorted telecom services, and is now climbing new hills on the Internet.

The point here is that you shouldn't only think in conventional terms. Technology opens up all sorts of opportunities. This isn't the race to run with blinders on.

Video Conferencing: A Picture is Worth a Thousand Words

Promises, promises. Purveyors of Video Conferencing (VC) equipment have long been promising the American business community that it would save us tons of money on corporate travel expenses. Well, it hasn't panned out that way—yet. The fact is, Video Conferencing is only marginally impacting business travel today. But don't blink. As prices of VC equipment continue to plummet, especially desktop VC units, more businesses are using it every day. In the next couple years, VC will be popping up in all sorts of businesses, large and small, like the fax machine did in the 1980s. As soon as enough people and businesses use VC with confidence and regularity, we'll see a corresponding drop in the need for business travel.

Let's face it, there is a real value to flying a thousand miles for a five-minute face-to-face meeting about a critically important matter with a major client. It demonstrates how important the other person, or the topic, is to you. But most brief business meetings aren't that important, and the virtual face-to-face achieved by way of a Video Conferencing system would work just as well as the in-person meeting.

The first business trips impacted by VC are intra-company travel. Say, for example, that you need to get together, on a regular basis, with one or more of your associates in different branch offices around the country. When you replace business travel with face-to-face VC meetings , your firm's travel budget can be reduced sharply, and you will save a lot of time.

Forward-thinking companies are already using intra-company VC to their advantage. Customer visits, on the other hand, are another story. That will take longer. Your customers will let you know when the time is right for them. Some are more "cutting-edge" than others. As they start using it in their businesses, they'll feel more comfortable doing business with you that way, too. But even if it takes a while to start cutting back on business travel, Video Conferencing can still enhance and personalize your everyday contact with your customers.

Unintended Benefits of Video Conferencing

While I was on a recent speaking engagement, an executive in the audience shared this story with me. He said his company recently installed Video Conferencing equipment in its key offices so that the far-flung research and development people could cut down on business travel, specifically the monthly meeting they'd all attend.

He related that the first video meeting was a disaster, because, apparently, they needed to be in the same room in order to scream at one another. The VC system didn't allow that degree of emotional interaction. For a while, he thought the new video equipment would be a total waste, but a funny thing started happening. In between their monthly in-person meetings, the team started having brief interim meetings using the conferencing equipment. Now, when they get together at the end of each month, they are light-years ahead of where they would have been without those extra video meetings. This cuts months, even years, off their product-development time, earning the company millions of dollars in extra revenues. The same potential exists for every business today.

It's easier than ever to get started with Video Conferencing. All it takes is a phone call to AT&T, MCI, Sprint or another long-distance company, or even your local phone company, for a turnkey solution. Or you can call VC manufacturers for the equipment and arrange for the lines separately.

With affordable, high-speed ISDN phone lines, you can use VC today from your home or the office. Newly emerging technology, however, is allowing desktop Video Conferencing to be used over plain local phone lines. This allows traveling executives to log into video conferences from wherever they are located—hotel room, airport lounge, branch office, wherever. All they need is a phone line and a laptop equipped with the right software and, of course, a little video camera.

Internet Video Conferencing is also catching on and is ready to explode into the marketplace. According to many analysts, the Internet will enable Video Conferencing to burst into the homes and offices of mainstream America. According to Andy Pargh, syndicated columnist and The Gadget Guru on NBC's *Today*

Show, Video Conferencing products are finally invading the consumer market. Manufacturers are shipping home versions of these video systems, which work with regular phone lines and existing TV sets with the addition of a set-top box and camera. The conversation is carried over phone lines, and the picture comes over your TV, along with the actual sound, which is broadcast over the TV speakers.

Public Video Conferencing terminals and setups are starting to pop up all over the place. Kinkos copy shops and Sprint have teamed up to offer Video Conferencing from their locations. Grandparents can talk face-to-face with their grandkids, located across the country, by simultaneously visiting their respective local Kinkos and buying some time on the VC system.

Virtual Conference Rooms are Catching on

Companies are holding meetings in hotels and conference centers equipped with Video Conferencing rooms. That way, employees from far-flung locations can gather for meetings without the expense and time of traveling. The subtleties are getting better, too. For instance, VC-equipped conference rooms in various locations are purposely appointed exactly alike, and the life-sized video screen is located at the end of the conference table. On screen you can see the extension of the table, but it's really at another location—maybe in another time zone. It just appears to be an extension of your table because it's supposed to give that illusion. According to an *Information Week* article, if done correctly, participants actually start to be lulled into thinking they are in the same room and, when the meeting adjourns, have been known to get up and attempt to shake hands with the folks a thousand miles away. This is something we'll have to get used to, to save embarrassment, if nothing else. This is a change in the way we perceive reality, or, as author Don Tapscott calls it, a paradigm shift.

The bigger point here is that the more we get used to Video Conferencing, the more we'll use it at home and in the office. Like the fax, it's a revolution you can't stop, so you might just as well jump on the bandwagon and use it to your advantage.

Video Conferencing Starting to Roar

Video Conferencing, in general, is getting ready for the big time. Researchers Frost & Sullivan predict market revenues will jump from $2.9 billion in 1995 to nearly $35 billion in 2002, which translates into an amazing 42.3% annual growth rate. These statistics are mirrored by those of the International Teleconferencing Association (ITCA), which reports North American VC revenues of $2.29 billion in 1995, an increase of almost 50% over its 1994 numbers. ITCA says there are currently about 100,000 two-way interactive Video Conferencing rooms and offices in North America. Rooms, not desktop sets. Add those individual users into the mix and you've got many times more.

Document Conferencing

Thanks to the advancements in desktop Video Conferencing, you can not only *see* the other party, but you can also be working together on the same document, on the computer screen, at the same time—working on contracts, scripts, plans, drawings, advertising, whatever. No longer does writer Tammy DeMarcus have to describe in detail what she is seeing, and editing, to the person at the other end of the phone line, who before would be frantically scanning her printed copy of the document, searching for the changes Tammy is describing. Now they both look at the document—at the same time, on-screen—using document-sharing software, and either one can make changes right on the document, which show up instantly on the other's screen. "This has changed and improved the way I work so much. It's as important to me as the fax machine," says DeMarcus.

Much of this book was done through a more crude form of document sharing. The publisher and I e-mailed chapters and revisions back and forth until we were both happy. This allowed us both to work on the book at our own pace and in our own time, and to simply hand it off to each other when sections were completed. In days past, chapters would have to be overnighted or even faxed. But having the documents already in computer text form allowed for cleaner, easier editing and revisions.

Real-time interaction—as though both parties are sitting at the same table making changes to the documents so the other could see—requires document-sharing technologies, but don't underestimate the power of simply sending documents back and forth when real-time interaction isn't necessary.

Wildfire Could Make Secretaries Obsolete

Most of us occasionally ponder the future, but that's Paul Saffo's full-time job. As a director at the Institute for the Future in Menlo Park, California, Saffo tracks the technologies we will be using tomorrow. Once in a while he gets lucky and finds tomorrow's technology available today. Such is the case with an amazing electronic Voice Messaging assistant called Wildfire. This product can actually take the place of a receptionist, and do almost everything but get your morning coffee. Think of Wildfire as voice mail on steroids.

The system is designed for business people who rely on the telephone, yet who often miss important calls when out of the office or because they're always on the phone. Wildfire uses voice recognition technology to actually converse with you. A pleasant female voice is your Wildfire assistant. She—I mean *it*—is always on-call when you are on the phone. All you have to do is say, "Wildfire," and she jumps in, "Here I am." The system answers your phone, takes messages when you are away, responds to your voice commands, reminds you of appointments, recognizes the voices of those who have called before (and says, "Oh hi!"), lets you leave messages for certain callers, sets up conference calls on the fly, and much more.

Wildfire even whispers in your ear if a new call comes in while you are "in session," and asks if you'd like it to put the call through or take a message. This way, you never miss important calls when you are constantly on your office phone, or standing at a pay phone, or using a hotel-room phone a thousand miles away from your office. Talk about an effective tool for battling telephone tag!

Wildfire is an effective marriage of the telephone, computer and voice recognition technologies. Some users liken it to the computer on the bridge of the Starship Enterprise. A Wildfire session begins when you pick up the phone in your office or call into Wildfire from the road.

Paul Saffo describes a typical Wildfire session: "On the way to the office, I can call into Wildfire from the car, and with one call listen to all my messages, return only the calls I choose by simply telling Wildfire to 'give them a call,' take new calls as they come in, record notes and more, without ever hanging up the phone and redialing, jotting any information down, or taking my eyes off the road. I do it all by talking to my Wildfire assistant. I can blow through all my messages in record time, with a minimum of effort. Wildfire keeps me in touch without giving up my privacy."

Incidentally, it's also a great way to beat the system on those airline in-flight phones. Now that some airlines charge a flat fee of $15 or so per call, you can simply call Wildfire once and then make and receive dozens of calls for the price of one, because you never hang up and redial.

Wildfire is available from communications service bureaus, which also offer voice mail, pagers, and other services. More importantly, the Wildfire developers are planning a strategic change in distribution channels, making it available as a network service directly from phone companies. Soon, you should be able to order it just like Call Waiting and Call Forwarding from many local, long-distance or wireless phone companies.

This technology is a perfect example of outside-the-box, breakthrough thinking. It's a new way of addressing old problems, and it's a way to *WOW* your customers. Want a demo? Call 1-800-WILDFIRE. It'll blow your socks off.

International Callback Saves Money

The U.S. has the most competitive telecommunications industry in the world—and the lowest-priced services. Because of this, overseas calling rates that originate in the U.S. are the cheapest in the world. A typical call from Europe to the U.S. costs about $1 to $2 per minute. The same call from the U.S. to Europe costs about $0.40 per minute. This wide discrepancy created an environment ripe for the spawning of a whole new industry: International Callback.

Here's how it works: Say you are visiting Paris and you want to call a client in Munich. The French phone company, a government-owned monopoly, is going to charge you a fortune for the call. It would be considerably cheaper to call Munich from the U.S., where the international rates are significantly lower. Enter the callback service. Using a pre-assigned, dedicated phone number, you dial your callback service, located in the States, and hang up after one ring. Because you hang up after only one ring, without actually completing the call, the local phone company cannot charge you for a completed call. However, that one ring is enough to signal the switch/computer that you called, seeking dialtone to set up a call.

Recognizing your pre-assigned call-in number, the switch/computer is programmed to immediately dial you back at the phone number you previously designated, referred to as your *callback number*. The callback number can be changed at any time, remotely, either by calling your callback service directly, using the local phone service, or by using an automated interactive menu, provided by your callback service, the next time you are online and using the callback service. The callback number you designate can be a customer's office, your hotel or your cellular phone.

You now have dialtone that originates in the U.S. Then you will be prompted by the switch/computer, using an automated IVR system, to enter the phone number you want to call in Munich. Once this is accomplished, the call is set up, consisting of two legs that both originate in the U.S: one to Paris and another to Munich. Even though you are paying for two calls, plus the fee charged by the callback service, the U.S. rates are so much lower than those charged by other countries that the overall savings range from 30% to 70%.

The foreign telephone monopolies hate international callback with a passion. Some have made such services illegal. Singapore passed a law banning the provision of callback services and was met by a firestorm of protest from its citizens, who are, ultimately, the people who benefit from the savings that international callback provides. Singapore was pressured to quickly revoke its ban for the benefit of its own people.

International callback has instigated backdoor international competition by U.S. carriers, driving down rates worldwide. In the late 1980s international rates averaged $3 to $4 per minute. Now they average between $1 to $2 per minute. A significant reduction that was instigated by an intrepid group of entrepreneurs who set up international callback services and marketed them to the world.

Although the main customers for these services are foreign companies, business people who travel abroad frequently can also benefit. Don Younkin (e-mail: *callback@safari.net*; Web: *www.safari.net/~deadwood/callback.html*), who actually sells "transparent" callback services, plans to take his cellphone with him when he travels to Europe. When he arrives, he will establish service with a European cellular carrier (one that offers wide coverage all over Europe), and use his callback service for most of his long-distance calls.

Younkin has also been busy marketing automatic dialers that provide transparent callback capabilities to foreign hotels. An automatic dialer is hooked into the hotel telephone system, and it recognizes, each time a guest places an outgoing long-distance call, when it would be cheaper to use the callback service. The dialer then automatically routes the call to the callback service, saving a considerable amount on long-distance charges. The money saved is either retained by the hotel or passed along to its guests. To the guest, the call is the same as any other international call: he merely dials a number and waits for the other party to answer.

Despite the fact that the U.S. Government has been getting pressure from the rest of the world to curtail international callback, the FCC has shown little sympathy for these countries or their overcharging telephone monopolies, effectively giving the green light to the predominantly U.S.-based callback industry. Although the FCC cooperates with the handful of countries that have declared callback illegal, its position is that callback using uncompleted call signalling—the main point of contention with foreign phone companies, where you call and hang up after one ring—violates neither U.S. domestic nor international law. The FCC's position, however, does not authorize U.S. callback providers to offer service to customers in countries that have expressly declared it to be illegal.

Where do you find a callback service? Check the Yellow Pages under "telecommunications services." Or enter the keyword *international callback* in one of the Internet search engines, and you will find dozens. Now some of the major phone companies are beginning to offer callback services. AT&T was once vehemently opposed to such services, but now offers the service to its customers.

Where to Find
All the New Communications Products

Many new technologies, phones, boxes, gadgets and gizmos improve the quality of your life and the productivity of your business. Where do you find sources for all this hardware? I've mentioned the phone companies for services, but hardware is a different story. There are many sources online and in your retail stores. Office supply warehouses such as Office Depot, Office Max and Staples are great sources.

If you really want to drool over the sheer variety and magnitude of selections, try Hello Direct (800-444-3556). By no means is Hello Direct the only company offering communications solutions, but it is a great place to start. It operates a mail-order business through traditional catalogs and also has put its catalogs online. Check out its Web site at *www.hello-direct.com*. It offers everything to make your life on the phone better and more productive. If you have a phone hardware problem, Hello Direct probably has a solution.

This is actually a good use of Web sites. If you are in the mail-order business and publish catalogs, you know how expensive it can be—not only for the actual catalog printing, but also for storing, shipping and mailing. Then you either run out of catalogs or you are stuck with piles of outdated ones when it's time to print a new edition. How inefficient. The Web fixes all these problems. You can update prices, change entries, make additions and deletions as needed, whenever needed, so your online catalog is always up to date, without the waste of traditional catalogs.

Even if you still need to have printed catalogs on hand, you won't need as many, since many users will be able to go online. And even if you run out, all you have to do is direct the customer to your Web page.

Keep Your Antenna Up

There are so many cutting-edge technologies—and countless ways that creative business people are leveraging them to make money and provide better service—that there is no way to name them all. This chapter, or, for that matter, this entire book, should not be looked at as a complete list. At best it's a snapshot of a few ways a handful of companies are making the technology work for them.

You already have the motivation to take advantage of the power in these tools or you wouldn't have this book in your hands right now. The best advice is to keep your radar up. Keep alert to what other businesses are using and how they are serving their customers better. These days, even the smallest business can take advantage of the power offered by the same technologies that, just a few years ago, only the largest companies could afford.

Keep alert for all the new tools that can make your life easier. All the honest-to-gosh better mousetraps, like one of my new personal favorites, the handheld digital voice recorder. Like its predecessor, the small, handheld micro-cassette recorder, you can record dictation, notes, ideas, letters, speeches, to-do lists, and whatever else you use the tape recorder for. But there is a powerful advantage to the newcomer. It's all digital, with no moving parts. Digital voice storage also gives it the same advantage voice mail has over a cassette-tape answering machine.

Voice mail lets you save or delete selected messages, rather than having to save or delete the entire tape, which is what an answering machine requires you to do. With these digital handheld recorders you can also save and delete selected messages. You can store messages in different folders. Here's an example: I keep notes for this book in one folder, and notes for my columns in another folder, and general notes in a third folder. I can then play, rewind, fast-forward, save or delete individual messages. I can also move them from one folder to another.

I used to hate having to transcribe my recorder notes because invariably I'd be looking for one piece of information buried somewhere in the tape. Now, I can quickly scroll through the messages one by one, listening to only the first moment of each message, to find what I am looking for. It has improved the efficiency of my note-taking a thousand percent.

I just discovered these little jewels, but they've been around for a year, at least. Only recently have they contained enough memory to be useful to me. They just keep getting more powerful. This is the power that's available today from countless other sources. Just keep your antenna up for all the new products and ideas. That's the smartest prescription.

Chapter 6
Electronic
Commerce Strategies

The Promise and the Peril

A profoundly ridiculous question being asked in the press and throughout the business community is, "Can I make money with the Internet?" This is like asking if you can make money with the telephone.

When the telephone was invented more than a century ago, who would have imagined telemarketing, call centers, 800 services and customer-service operations? The telephone has turned into one of the most powerful tools for marketing, sales and service. The Internet has all that going for it, and more. It's interactive, with both audio and video, and it can be designed to fulfill virtually any marketing and communications roles we can think of—and many we haven't dreamed of yet.

It no longer takes us a century to develop value from new technologies, either. The pace of change, and acceptance of new technologies, is accelerating. It took us less than 10 years to integrate the cellular telephone and the fax machine into the way we do business. It has taken only a few years for e-mail addresses to show up on business cards, and for World Wide Web addresses to pop up in ads and on product packaging.

And the Internet is still in its infancy. Only a few years ago we were debating whether to commercialize the Net, or leave it to academics and researchers from education and the government. For decades the Net was a simple, text-based informational tool. It has been only in the last couple of years that it has taken on a user-friendly, colorful, graphical interface, thanks in large part to the influx of fresh ideas and creativity from the business community.

I recently spoke at *Communications Week* magazine's Networked Economy conference in Washington, D.C. This allowed me to listen to and chat with folks like Don Tapscott, author of *Paradigm Shift*; Steve Case from America Online, and the CEOs and presidents of companies like Lucent, Netscape, Oracle, Sun Microsystems, AT&T Labs, Sprint, Cisco, Cascade, Bay Networks, and others. The leaders and architects of our changing economy. It was two days of ideas, visions and challenges surrounding electronic commerce, and the new rules for doing business. Rules that are impacting all businesses, large and small.

The Internet, e-mail and advancements in electronic commerce are changing the way products and services are bought and sold. Traditional storefronts, with their geographically-limited market areas, are rapidly giving way to home pages and electronic storefronts, which enable even the smallest businesses to look like their larger competitors. But more than that, this enables them to compete and market products and services nationally, even globally, instead of being limited to their traditional little corners of the world. This is opening up whole new frontiers for businesses of all sizes to conquer.

Not only is electronic commerce changing the way we do business, it's also changing the way wealth is created, rewriting the rules of our economy. According to Don Tapscott, who also wrote *The Digital Economy*, the developed world is evolving from an industrial-based economy to a digital-based economy. Silicon and computer networks are replacing steel, highways and automobiles as the drivers of this new economy. Analysts, business leaders and politicians agree. We are going through a profound change of historic proportions. Changes that cannot be ignored.

Instead of resisting the change so that we can continue to do things the way we've always done them, we should consider this a time of unprecedented opportunity. Whenever change on this scale has occurred before, it has also created phenomenal new opportunities. We should be spending our energies searching for those new opportunities. Fortunately, we don't have to look far. Most opportunities are hidden just beneath the foam of the turbulent waters whipped up by the swift, relentless change we are experiencing.

Can you make money on the Net? Can you make money with telephones? Accept the Internet for what it is: a powerful communications tool that will transform the way we do business. Just like the telephone and the automobile did a century ago. Our grandparents adapted, and we must do the same, in a much shorter period of time.

Opportunities Abound for Opportunists

Success in the new marketplace will go to the opportunist. Be vigilant for changing customer needs and trends. Be nimble enough to adapt to those needs, and swift enough to pounce on them before they change yet again.

Today's opportunities may not be as long-lived as in days past. That's why being a perpetual opportunist is the answer. Always have your radar up to take advantage of the avalanche of ideas and opportunities that present themselves every day in newspaper headlines and news stories.

Electronic banking, e-cash, e-mail, electronic marketing, Internets, intranets, call centers and the like are the wave of the future. Over the next several years electronic commerce will rapidly become a key way through which many people will be buying and selling your products and services.

This is not a passing fad.

This is even beyond a trend.

It's a shift. A shift in the way we do things and the way we *think* about doing things. We no longer have to travel *there* to get what we want. We no longer have to be limited by store hours or geography. In fact, with electronic commerce, there often is no *there*, there.

$10 Billion by the Year 2000 or Bust

The Yankee Group forecasts consumer Internet commerce growing from $730 million in 1996 to $10 billion in 2000. It's also important to note that in 1995 Internet commerce was pegged at less than $200 million, and only $50 million the year before. The growth is astounding. And it illustrates how fast this phenomenon is occurring, and how important it is that you start getting your feet wet with these new technologies, new channels to reach customers, and new ways of doing business.

Many banks, florists, book stores and assorted sales organizations, big and small, are already blazing new trails by having a virtual storefront on the Internet, and leveraging the new technologies. Many don't have a physical storefront at all. Government agencies are quickly getting in on the act, too. Not only can you get a wealth of information online with a few clicks of the mouse, but you are already able to file taxes electronically. In the next couple years, you won't even be getting checks from the IRS. Your refund will be transferred right into your bank account. Soon, you'll be able to vote, renew your driver's license, and get a business license.

You'll no longer be forced to jump in the car and drive across town, only to wait in a long line, to accomplish the many chores that inevitably intrude on our daily lives.

Reality check: While many businesses are being started from scratch in the electronic marketplace, most businesses are integrating the new ways into their existing operations. They are experimenting with the Internet, home pages, intranets, and so on, melding them into their present marketing formulas. By integrating them into their traditional telemarketing, call centers and marketing activities, they are generating and fulfilling more orders than ever.

Fruit Stand Caught in the Web

Last year, I wrote about Barry Gainer in *Success* magazine. Gainer owns Indian River Gift Fruit Company in Titusville, Florida. Early on, Gainer recognized the power of the Internet for marketing. He opened a storefront on the Internet (*http://www.giftfruit.com*) and on America OnLine, where the keyword *fruit* takes you to his AOL site. To encourage people to come back and revisit his site, he posts nutritional information and recipes on the fruits they sell, and even offers a virtual grove tour. "You've got to be creative to keep people coming back," says Gainer.

Gainer was convinced to go into the family's orange-growing business. Seeing lots of potential, he decided what the family business needed were some fresh marketing and promotion ideas. He was right. After reading about the Internet and online services, Gainer decided this was more than a passing fad and decided to open a storefront in cyberspace. He didn't expect to make money right away, but he now reports that he's doing just that. Early in 1996 his online business was taking roughly 100 new orders per week resulting from around 9,000 hits per month on his Web site, which is phenomenal—and that's during the slow season. In early 1997, he was up to 300 orders per week, with a goal of 1,000 per week. At that rate, he'll reach his goal in a year or two. "Twenty-five percent of our business now comes from the Net and AOL," says Gainer.

Electronic commerce has excelled in his case. Gainer has even hired new employees to staff an online marketing department. They cruise the Internet answering questions about fruits, recipes, gifts, and so on. The "sig" line alone is great advertising, and it's all free. The sig line—Internet lingo for signature line—is simply a tag line you can automatically add to the end of all your e-mail or forum messages. It's like an electronic letterhead with your name, company name, slogan or anything else you want to include.

Tip: Make it easy for people to find you. Create *hot links* to other home pages that attract similar Net surfers. Encourage other homes pages to put links to your page. Weave a web to catch as many of the right visitors as possible. Also, make sure you list your site with the major search engines. This way, you get more visits, more traffic, and more bang for your buck. New software packages automate this task for you, logging on and listing your site with search engines. Automation is making everything easier as each week goes by. Even if something is difficult to do today, take heart. For it, too, will be automated before long.

Jewelry Store Strikes Gold on Internet

Jeweler Steve Quick told *Crains Small Business* that he created DiamondSource, a virtual diamond store on the Web, as an adjunct to his retail store. DiamondSource sells certified diamonds to individuals and other jewelers around the country. "We're receiving three or four requests for information a day, and about one-third of the calls turn into sales. The Web has paid for itself and more," says Quick.

Need I say more?

Old Time Specialty Shop, New Fangled Technology

"Virtual Vineyards is a high-tech version of an old-style specialty shop," says Peter Granoff, co-founder and proprietor, "where the proprietor greets each customer by name and is familiar with his or her individual tastes and preferences." This is the concept and vision that makes Virtual Vineyards so popular on the Web. Located at *www.virtualvin.com*, it sells fine foods and wines on the Internet.

The difference between Virtual Vineyards and others is that it doesn't simply sell its wares online, it also creates an engrossing online shopping experience. You wouldn't just throw up a store, stock the shelves and open the doors, Granoff says. You'd design a pleasant experience for the customer. The same care should be taken on the Web.

Cyberspace is Booming

Never before has a new technology been embraced by the American business community as has the Internet. Just a few years ago, we were debating whether or not to commercialize the Net. In just three years, businesses with a home page on the Internet's World Wide Web (WWW) exploded from less than a thousand to more than 100,000—and the rate of growth is increasing. Businesses of all sizes are opening storefronts on the Internet. And why not? Millions of potential customers are "surfing the Net," poised to visit and shop at your "store," and many more are on the way.

Today, only those with computers and modems are on the Internet. In the next few years, as computers get easier to use, more and more people will be using them at home and in the office. In fact, an important trend is developing. The American family is spending more time in front of the computer and less in front of the television, according to "The Lexmark Report on Computing and the American Family." The study, conducted by Roper Starch

Worldwide, looked at 1,000 households in which there was a computer. According to Nick Tortorello, senior vice president of Roper Starch, "Just as the hearth acted as the focal point for the American family in the 19th century, the television was the focus in the 20th century, and computer units are becoming the centerpiece for the American family in the 21st century."

This finding is confirmed by several studies. This bodes ill for the major television networks, which are already scrambling to re-tool for the 21st century with such entries as MSNBC and CNBC, the Internet and Cable TV reincarnations of their network selves. But it also opens up new worlds of opportunity for smart and forward-thinking marketers.

The Internet is also becoming accessible through cable TV, smart phones, and so on. As this unfolds, reaching critical mass in the mass market is imminent. A huge consumer market of tens of millions—or even hundreds of millions—of Internet visitors will open up almost overnight. This is happening as we speak.

That's when the businesses that are experimenting with the Internet, now, as a marketing medium, will find themselves doing more business in cyberspace than they ever imagined. That's what Mr. Gainer is striving for. He wants to grow his firm into the biggest gift-fruit shipper in Florida. But more importantly, businesses that are not getting online today will find themselves in a mad dash tomorrow to get there, and they'll be making mistakes they should be making now, when it's okay because everybody else is in the same learning mode.

How Many People Will Really Be on the Internet?

The rate of growth of the Internet is astounding. "If you look at the numbers and the rate of growth and project it out over the next few years," jests Vinton Cerf, " it looks like every living soul on the planet will be using the Internet." Cerf, widely considered the father of the Internet and now vice president of MCI's Internet operation, may be only half-kidding.

Are businesses making money on the Internet? In 1995 and 1996, only a few were, but now, with increasing frequency, businesses are finding gold online. However, there is still consumer fear of using credit-card numbers on the Web. "Many people underestimate the general reluctance to buy through the Net," says Marcia Yudkin, author of *Marketing Online*. Yudkin favors more traditional online activities like networking and "online schmoozing."

However, such reluctance may be evaporating. Security on the Net is improving and people are becoming accustomed to doing business this way. The more customers get used to the idea, the more business they will do online. Encryption software and other security measures are already in place, and it's only a matter of time before safe financial transactions become the norm.

Shopping Online, But Buying in Person or Via 800

A Nielsen Media Research study concluded that doing business on the Internet is finally heating up and moving beyond the novelty stage. The study found that 73% of the 50 million World Wide Web users spend a portion of their online time searching for product or service information. However, the Internet is used primarily for browsing and shopping at this stage, not purchasing. Only 15% are actually purchasing online; the rest gather information and shop for what they want, then place the order with a credit card over the telephone, usually through an 800 number.

Even if that remains the Internet's biggest contribution to electronic commerce—shopping and information-gathering, but buying in more traditional ways—it's still a significant benefit and an incredible marketing tool for any size business. However, Internet shopping is still new and buying resistance is steadily weakening. Before long, the number of actual purchase transactions may rival those of telephone orders.

Greg Renker, CEO and genius behind the mail-order and direct-marketing firm Gunthy-Renker, recently told CNNfn that there's a consumer segment that loves to shop via the Internet. These shoppers can get any level of detail necessary to make the purchase and then, by the simple press of a button, order the product and have it delivered to their doorsteps. Gunthy-Renker, which has been successful in the infomercial game, has staked out its claim in cyberspace by launching an online retailing channel called America's Choice Mall.

E-Cash

Not only is our method of doing business changing, but our monetary system is going to be going through some pretty profound changes as well. The networked, digital economy is crying out for a safe, secure, easy way to pay for goods and services online.

Traditional cash and credit are at best clumsy on the Net. Credit cards work adequately for tens of thousands of businesses that process such transactions online, but that's thinking about tomorrow's marketplace in yesterday's terms. It's like having to walk around in the 1800s with a pocket full of five-dollar coins because paper money was scarce back then. There is a growing demand for a currency that is designed from the outset especially for the networked economy.

Enter e-cash. Many of the nation's top financial institutions—such as GTE CyberTrust, MasterCard, Visa, VeriFone, CheckFree and others—are working to develop systems that offer electronic currency for online transactions. Much of the work revolves around digital certificates, or coins, with a public and a private key (or code), developed by people experienced in cryptography. The security is high since the certificate cannot be used without both keys.

Most systems are essentially software based, where e-cash is stored on your computer's hard drive, in an e-cash account that can be spent and replenished as necessary. Without getting too deep into the topic, which is evolving as you read these words, suffice it to say that just as the business community adopted checks and credit cards years ago, it will also eventually adopt a new kind of currency and payment system in order to facilitate commerce on the Internet. Electronic commerce is going to be too big and too important—too quickly—to continue using the modern-day equivalent of bear skins and stone knives. Necessity drives innovation in a free market, and e-cash on hard drives will inevitably become as common as dollar bills in wallets.

Buying Online Should be Easy, Fun and Interactive

Think of the online experience for your customers as an extension of your other marketing efforts, like toll-free 800 numbers, direct mail and mail order. In its basic form the online experience is simply another way to reach customers using the power of images and sounds together. TV consists of pictures and sounds too, but the Net is interactive. Customers can get as much or as little information on any particular product or service as they choose, at a pace controlled by them alone.

They should be able to simply go to your site, find the products and services you sell, shop among your offerings, get as much in-depth information as they need on anything you offer, and then buy what they want with a few clicks of a button.

As more customers and businesses get used to the new e-cash and digital certificates, buying will get even easier. Not that it's all that difficult now. Today it's as simple as entering your credit card information on an online order form. Then *viola*, the order is placed and the item is on its way. The good part is that customers get to see, read and hear all the information they need to make an informed purchase decision. That's the beauty and the power of the interactive nature of the Net.

Researchable Businesses Do Well on the Web

According to the Yankee Group, consumer Internet commerce appears to be dominated by what it calls researchable industries, such as travel, computer hardware, software and consumer electronics. This makes sense. These purchases require more investigation, education and comparison than buying a tube of toothpaste. The Internet makes it easy to learn more about these products while shopping around for the best deal.

Small Companies are Blazing New Trails—Big Companies are Watching Closely

Small businesses see the Internet as the great equalizer—a huge new opportunity to reach new markets and level the playing field. On the Internet, any business can look as impressive or as modest as it wants to. These small businesses, unhindered by conservatism or layers of management and bureaucracy, are jumping onto the Net, leveraging new opportunities, and making early progress.

However, while the small companies are the trailblazers, the bigger competitors are watching closely. When they are ready, they'll pounce onto the Web. Amazon.com is a case in point. Launched in 1995 by Jeff Bezos, it's one of the hottest retailers on the Web. A virtual bookstore, it calls itself "Earth's Biggest Bookstore" and, with about 2.5 million titles, it well might be. Bezos told the *Wall Street Journal* that revenues have been leaping by 20% to 30% each month, and the payroll has increased from seven employees to almost 250 in less than two years. This is phenomenal, but holding onto the lead might be tougher in the years ahead.

Industry heavyweights Barnes and Noble, Simon & Schuster, and others, seeing the Internet as a viable conduit through which to reach customers, and bolstered by the success of Amazon.com, are rushing to the Web with super sites of their own. Steve Riggio, Barnes & Noble's chief operating officer, told *Information Week* that they will have deeper discounts than any other retailer. Them's fightin' words out there in the land of marketing.

That means Amazon.com will have to think of new and creative ways to use the power of the Web to attract and retain customers and continue its amazing growth. Bezos says most people just don't focus on the customer and their Web experience enough. This is the strength of the entrepreneurial mind. They are not afraid to try new and even quirky ideas.

Amazon.com takes full advantage of the unique interactive features of the Web in delivering a new experience to the customer. For example, customers can search for books by author, title or subject. Or they can browse through certain subject categories, just like bookstore shelves. A powerful search engine will list books by subject or by the key word entered. Each individual title listing has sections for reader reviews, author comments and publisher remarks—information that is entered by these people at any time when visiting the Web site. For example, the author might discuss why he wrote the book, and the publisher might include an excerpt or a noteworthy review by the media. This is all voluntary information that can be entered or changed at any time by filling out standard fill-in-the-blank e-mail forms on the Web site itself.

Amazon.com also offers a personalized search feature called "Eyes," which lets readers specify a title, subject or author and then automatically receive e-mail notification when a new book is published that matches their requirements. The Web takes personalized retailing into new territory.

And look at the numbers. Regular bookstores might stock some 20,000 titles. The big super bookstores carry some 60,000 titles.

Amazon.com offers 2.5 million, including books from obscure publishers with no hope of ever getting bookstore distribution. And nearly half of those are out-of-print books that will never show up in a regular bookstore, no matter what the size.

Amazon.com is also pioneering new selling methods. "I'd rather enlist 100 people to sell one thing each, than try to sell 100 things myself," is a quote often attributed to Andrew Carnegie. Looks like Amazon.com has figured out the power of that secret. It offers a program where other businesses can sell books from their Web pages by putting a link to Amazon.com for the actual order fulfillment, earning a commission on each sale. Everybody wins. The participating company (or individual) can make sales without handling inventory or order processing. Amazon.com can enlist a huge cyber sales force that will multiply its presence on the Web and sell more books. This is the kind of new, breakthrough thinking it takes to succeed in the new marketplace.

What will be the next hot ideas? Your guess is as good as mine. But in the online world, *the quirkier the better* seems to be the mantra. Anything to break through the clutter. And Bezos has a lofty goal of being in the top three book brands in the country and a billion-dollar business by the year 2000. That seems like a stretch in yesterday's terms, until you consider the incredible growth the company is experiencing, as well as the growth of the Web itself. According to the *New York Times*, Amazon.com is one of the few Internet marketers that is earning substantial revenues. The company served some 340,000 customers in more than 100 countries in less than two years. More than 40 percent of those customers are repeat buyers—worth their weight in gold to any retailer. The battle for online book sales business is heating up. How about your business?

Remember: What's good for the goose is also good for the gander. Small businesses are learning just as much from larger companies on how to market on the Web. Many larger companies have excellent Web sites, and much can be learned from watching everyone's follies on the Net. Watching other businesses and going to school on their experiences is the cheapest, most effective course in Internet and electronic commerce available today.

Sell Advertising on Your Web Site

Marketing your products or services on the Internet isn't the only way to make money with the computer network. If you have a popular site that lots of people visit, then consider selling advertising. Advertisers pay for exposures, or "hits," on the Internet. Search engines like Yahoo make their money in exactly this way. Visit any popular site and you'll see paid advertising.

It's a great way for a marketer to target an audience, based on specific, definable interests. Big money is being spent on advertising, and advertisers love to focus their message to the exact target audience that is most likely to buy their products. The Internet does just that. Why not cash in? According to AdSpend data released by Jupiter Communications, an Internet and online research firm, total U.S. online advertising was estimated at $301 million in 1996.

Roughly $260 million went to Web sites, and $41 million went to non-Web services like America OnLine, PointCast, and so on. The growth in advertising continues, as does the growth of the Internet itself. Sure, $301 million is a drop in the bucket compared to the total of other traditional advertising expenditures, but remember that the Internet didn't exist, in any meaningful commercialized form, just a few years ago. Advertising on the Internet is a new advertising venue. In that light, a few hundred million dollars is a terrific coming-out party.

Marketers are always looking for the most accurately-targeted media that reaches their best prospects. All businesses want to spend their advertising dollars as cost-effectively as possible. Huge sums of money are wasted on advertising to people who do not want to buy what is being sold. Either they are not interested or the time isn't right. Your Web site will attract people belonging to a certain demographic profile, based on the content of your site. Your visitors are likely to be good potential buyers of products related to your site, and the makers of those products will be interested in advertising with you if you are pulling in heavy traffic.

This is called "rifle shot" advertising, because the message is delivered to a precisely-targeted group of prospects. The alternative is "shotgun blast" advertising, were the message is broadcast to everyone in the hopes that at least a few may be persuaded to buy. Direct mail to carefully-selected mailing lists or ads in specialized trade publications are also rifle shot ads. Newspaper and TV ads are shotgun blasts. Rifle shot is invariably better when selling specialized items to a definable market. It better focuses the advertising dollars to the people most likely to buy. Marketers recognize the value of such ads and will pay for them.

Intranets are the Next Wave

Just when you're getting used to the Internet, it has already spawned offspring. Intranets are now bursting onto the scene. Think of an intranet as a restricted, secure version of the Internet, for use within only one company. An intranet is accessible only to those with permission and access codes—customers, employees and affiliates.

Companies use intranets to communicate, share and distribute information when the Internet isn't as appropriate. The closed nature of intranets affords better security and less chance of hackers making spaghetti of your computer networks. Even though you may not have heard much about intranets, chances are you'll be using one of your customer's or supplier's intranets within the next year, and perhaps starting your own shortly after that.

People like the Web for its colorful point-and-click graphics and text, and for its ability to whisk you to whatever information you want in the blink of an eye. The Web links tens of thousands of different computers in virtually every country on earth. Intranets use this same attractive, point-and-click graphical environment, but for internal company communications and information exchange. You can develop your own internal home-page-like site in addition to, or instead of, your own Web home page.

Using the same off-the-shelf HTML (Hyper Text Markup Language) software used for Internet home page design, you can design your own communications, information and messaging center through which to share information—both internally and externally—with employees, customers and suppliers. A good example is Atlanta-based Georgia Pacific, which is using an intranet to link its 56,000 employees who are scattered around the world. It is implementing this intranet technology to improve its communications and to distribute information. GP implemented its massive intranet network over a two-year period. Small companies, wanting to act and look larger, can implement a modest version that can be up and running quickly and relatively inexpensively.

Some of the benefits of intranets are:

❑ Employees can work on projects collaboratively, from geographically-dispersed locations, through groupware-type software.

❑ Catalogs and price lists can be put online and changed as often as needed to keep them current—without the massive expense of frequent printing and mailing.

❑ Sales reps can close more business by having real-time access to product specs and documentation—connecting with modem and laptop right from the customer's location—enabling them to strike while the iron is hot.

❑ Orders can be placed electronically by your customers 24 hours a day.

❑ Customer service can be provided 24 hours a day, seven days a week.

❑ Frequently-requested information and documents can be available online.

❑ Video and audio clips can be made available, offering superior product demonstrations.

❑ Telecommuting can be enabled, allowing people to work anytime, anyplace, with access to company information—just like they were in the office.

❑ Virtually any information need can be addressed quickly and disseminated relatively inexpensively.

❑ And, of course, intranets can be linked to the Internet for seamless communicating across the global network.

MCI, Microsoft and Digital Equipment Corp announced in a high-profile joint press conference that they are combining to offer these enhanced intranet and Internet services, so you don't have to feel like you are going it alone. If Digital Chairman Bob Palmer, MCI Chairman Bert Roberts, and Microsoft Chairman Bill Gates are getting together and betting on a horse, it's not wise to bet against them. Computer companies report that in past years 80% of their customer-service calls came through their 800 lines. Today, 80% of these customer service calls come in over the Internet or through their intranets.

Extranets: Like *Deja Vu* All Over Again

Extranets, the newest kids on the online block, are similar to intranets, but are designed for secure transactions and communications among *several* companies. However, they still don't operate in an open environment, like the Internet. They are somewhere between the Internet and intranets—more secure than the Internet, allowing only certain users, but used by several participating organizations.

Kenneth Horner, principal for information technology for Deloitte & Touche Consulting Group, told *Industry Week*, "Traditional manufacturing/distribution chains stand to benefit quite a bit from an extranet approach. You really have to change the way you do business. It's as fundamental a change as the introduction of the telephone or the fax machine." No question, these are the new tools for the future.

Internet? Intranet? Extranet? Which?

Which is right for your company? Depending on your business, maybe one, maybe all. It's like asking which is right for your company—telephone, fax machine, mail delivery, or overnight delivery? They are all new tools for a new generation of doing business. Within a few years, you will likely be using them all. I can't say which is the best place to start. All I can do is impress upon you the importance of starting—getting up to speed with these new technologies. Your competitors are!

The Internet:
Not Just for Home Pages Anymore

Thinking about the Internet in terms of home pages and interactive sites is like saying your home is for sleeping only. In both cases, you're recognizing only part of the value and beneficial uses. The Internet is developing into much more than just a place to have a virtual storefront. It's becoming the core of the new communications and information revolution. Many new technologies and tools—available on the Internet and via online services—have nothing to do with home pages. For example, software companies make their software updates available for downloading, either free or through a secure site, saving considerable money in shipping costs. Read on for other examples.

Competitive and Market Research Made Easy

Want to keep up with news and trends in your industry? Follow the announcements and actions of your competitors? Track the activities of other industry executives? Well, you've come to the right place. The Internet and various online news wires, newspapers, magazines, online services and databases hold a bounty of valuable information waiting to be mined. As in any gold mine, however, you've got to dig through lots of other stuff to get to the gold.

The dozen or so largest search engines on the Internet—Yahoo, AltaVista and others—are great places to start. Simply enter the key words on the subjects about which you want information. Company names, individuals names, product names, whatever. Up comes a listing of information sources, some of which are irrelevant, but a scan of the top ten or 20 items will give you what you're looking for, or at least narrow your search.

Competitive and market research has never been easy or quick. But now, instead of spending days or weeks in various libraries and information repositories, you can find what you need while sitting at your keyboard, anytime of the day or night, in minutes or hours.

Government agencies and bureaus are also a great source of information. The government spends billions every year researching everything. And more government information is going online every day. Check out the Library of Congress at *http://lcweb.loc.gov* or the *Thomas Register*, named after Thomas Jefferson, at *http://thomas.loc.gov/*. These are some of the most comprehensive sites on the Net. You will also find plenty of links to other government sites. Links that can get you to the information you want, now.

Every day millions of Americans spend countless hours on hold waiting to get information from government offices. Now, much of that information and research is available online. With a few keystrokes, you can now get in a few minutes what used to take days, waiting for the mail to arrive.

Colleges and universities, among the first to inhabit the Internet, often have decades worth of material on their sites. Visit the online libraries and research databases of the worlds great libraries. Simply type the name of any university you would like to explore into a search engine like AltaVista or Yahoo, and you'll find more information from these academic sites than you can imagine.

Private companies also load their sites with mountains of valuable information in order to attract visitors like you. They do it for marketing reasons, and you can use the information for competitive research. It's amazing. Companies that are otherwise tight-fisted with information, for competitive reasons, load their Internet sites with all sorts of historical information and data on their company and their industry. You can often get access to annual reports, financial data, business strategy information, archives of press releases, product announcements and the text of executive speeches. Just by scouring the Internet for these kinds of sites you can get an incredible storehouse of information. But there are even more sources of competitive and market research.

Other Online Research Resources

The online database Profound holds market research reports, which are available from any keyboard. For a monthly subscription fee, you are free to search its deep database of market reports, research and surveys from many of the big market-research firms. You can either purchase an entire report or any section that is relevant to your needs. If you purchase only parts of a report, you only pay for those sections. This information is available on its proprietary online version, or on its Internet version at *www.profound.com.*

News wires like Reuters, Associated Press, Dow Jones and others are also online. Newspapers like the *Wall Street Journal, USA Today* and the *New York Times* are online. Magazines like *Business*

Week, *Fortune* and *Forbes* are online, as are trade journals and industry newsletters.

John F. Kennedy reportedly read a half-dozen newspapers every morning, which was quite an accomplishment back in 1960. Today, I read the equivalent of dozens of newspapers and magazines every day and in less time than President Kennedy took to read his half-dozen. Lots of professionals do the same these days. How? By scanning online news sources that selectively provide the information you specify, tailored to your interests. In addition, by entering key words into their search features, you can make sure not to miss important news of the day on any topic.

Another powerful tool is the "search" or "archive" feature of these news sources. Most online publications provide access to years of articles and stories. Some charge for this access; others are free. Either way, they offer, in minutes, the benefits of spending weeks at the biggest library in the world. They do all the laborious searching, sifting and sorting.

How long would it take you to search the last three years worth of *Business Week* articles to find stories on your competitor? Hours? Days? Maybe weeks? How about less than five seconds online? Got your attention? Good, that's the point. Forget yesterday's way of doing things. Use today's tools. You wouldn't take an old biplane on a business trip, so why use ancient methods for doing business? For our purposes here, ancient is five or 10 years old when you're talking about technology.

Time has new meaning in the '90s. That's a key reality we need to grasp and accept. The pace of change is quickening. It took 10 years for cellphones to catch on. It took less for faxing. It has taken only a few years for e-mail, and video conferencing is coming on fast. We can't count on taking our sweet time to change what we do. We need to change as fast as change itself. Continually reinvent the processes our companies follow. If we don't, our competitors will, and then we'll be forced to respond on their terms. Either way it will happen. The only question is, will we be blazing the new trails, or following reluctantly behind the leader?

All this news and information searching takes time, and time is something most business people have in limited supply. The answer is to have the intelligence of the computer networks do the work for you. Smart agents of a sort. Let them scour the online world for you and bring back to you the relevant news and information you need.

An increasing variety of aids help automate this task. The results are either clipped and saved in electronic folders, like CompuServe's Executive News Service (ENS), for your later review; or sent to you via e-mail in daily editions through services like MCI's infoMCI or Individual, Inc.'s Heads Up service. "I use CompuServe's ENS to search the media while I sleep," says Thomas Antion, professional speaker and president of the National Capital Speakers Association. "This saves me lots of library research and gives me more up-to-date info on my client."

PointCast is another gem of a service. By going to the PointCast home page (*www.pointcast.com*) and downloading the program, you can customize a new service based on your interests. It gets news from CNN, *New York Times*, *Wired* magazine and loads of other national and local publications. It clips the stories you want to see based on your input when you personalize the service. It then periodically logs on to the Internet and downloads regular updated news and information to your computer. You then simply go to the PointCast software to read the new stories.

PointCast also serves as a screen-saver; instead of seeing flying windows or other designs, the news headlines flash by. Clicking on any headline will give you the full story. This is a powerful tool with which to scan the daily news and monitor certain companies and industries. And best of all, it's free. Revenues are generated from ad sales, so PointCast wants as many people using the service as it can get. So enjoy.

Freeloader (*www.freeloader.com*), like PointCast, offers personalized news and information from the 2,500 topics on Individual Inc.'s NewsPages. It also goes to the Web sites you've selected and downloads the new information so you can access it later, at your convenience, without having to go online and wait for slow downloads.

It does the surfing work for you, and saves everything to your hard-drive for quick and easy access at your convenience. This way, you can read news from AP Newswire, *Computerworld*, *Ad Age*, *Los Angeles Times*, *Washington Post*, *Information Week*, and more. With these tools, you can read news and information about others in your industry, get hot ideas, and implement them in your market area before your competition does.

Don't Reinvent the Wheel

Last year, after giving a speech in California, a local auto dealership owner came up to me to share this telling story. He told me about an Atlanta-area dealership that was breaking the rules and winning. Automobile advertising is traditionally focused on newspapers, and the Atlanta dealership decided to break from the pack and put most of its ad budget into TV. It worked, and the company grew faster and captured a bigger market-share than ever before. The dealer who told this story decided that if it worked once, it could work again, so he, too, shifted his advertising to TV. He was delighted to report that he had the same happy results.

This story is not simply that of a competitor copying a winning strategy. It's a story of a West Coast dealer going online and reading about an idea that worked on the East Coast. The story never appeared in any local paper or in other usual media. By using the Internet on a regular basis the owner is able to read such news stories from around the country, follow trends, and get new ideas to implement long before they become commonplace. This gives him a huge jump over his local competition. Any business person can follow this strategy and win. All sorts of success stories can be tapped into and integrated into your business. Ideas, information and inspiration are yours for the taking.

There are also online resources that will give you loads of off-the-shelf information on any major company. Try Hoovers Online at *www.hoovers.com* or access the site through any online service.

A great source of magazines with searchable archives is *www.pathfinder.com*. Don't forget that by simply typing the key words *research*, *competitive research* or *competitive intelligence* into any of the Internet search engines, you'll get loads of information sources. Talk about information overload!

Sell Information: E-mail Newsletters

Not only are large newspapers and magazines offering online versions of their publications, but specialized newsletters are also finding a whole new world to conquer. There are tens of millions of potential subscribers to newsletters in hundreds of specialized fields, markets, industries, trades, and interest groups too numerous to mention. Traditionally, newsletters have been mailed to subscribers. In recent years, urgent or timely letters have been faxed. While quality was lower, immediacy was unparalleled. And now, newsletters are being sent via e-mail, usually as long, simple text messages where the newsletter is actually within the body of the e-mail message. Another option is to create the newsletter in a word-processing program, save it as a file, and attach the file to an e-mail message. The newsletter is then transmitted to a mailing list of e-mail addresses. When received, the subscriber simply double-clicks on the file, which then appears on screen in readable form. It's inexpensive, immediate, and offers the best of all worlds.

Ken Leebow, the CPA who started a voice mail service bureau, was bitten by the Internet bug last year. He immersed himself in cyberspace, seeing what worked and what didn't, and why, and started publishing an e-mail newsletter. In about a year he has gained tens of thousands of subscribers. He charges a small subscription fee and sells ads. While he's not getting rich yet, it's certainly more than worth his while—but more importantly, he's getting his feet wet. Learning what readers want, like, and don't like. Making mistakes now when it's okay to make mistakes. A sample copy of the newsletter, which focuses on doing business on the Internet, can be acquired by sending an e-mail message to *TheLeebowLetter@mailback.com*. An auto responder, which will immediately and automatically send you back the sample copy, is another great tool for marketing. It's like a fax-back service for e-mail. Once you set up shop with an Internet site, you can take advantage of plenty of powerful features like this.

Internet Phones: From Novelty to Mainstream Communications

Only recently, making phone calls over the Internet was little more than an amusing side attraction—a novelty for people who like to play with high-tech wizardry. However, it didn't take long for this fun but clunky version of Internet telephony to catch the attention of telephone companies and Internet Service Providers (ISPs) alike. All the major phone companies have begun to announce the integration of the Internet and their traditional voice and data network offerings. This blending makes sense from many perspectives, so expect your phone companies to offer all sorts of voice/data deals that entwine the Internet with their more traditional offerings.

On a pair of fronts, Internet telephony has caught the imagination of many entrepreneurs and start-ups. On one hand, it's a great way to cut costs, even though its quality and reliability falls far short of that of the public telephone network. On the other hand, this is another cutting-edge technology that is bound to be big in the next few years. One of the many new and innovative opportunities to launch a new business and make some money. "So many pots of gold are out there just waiting for someone with enough guts to cross over the rainbow to claim," one entrepreneur told me.

FCC Chairman Reed Hundt Chairman says flatly that he doesn't want the old telephony rules to choke off this emerging technology and market. He and the FCC are doing everything in their power to get out of the way and let the Internet and Internet telephony develop its full potential.

When Internet phones first came onto the market, quality was marginal. Both parties on a conversation needed the same software loaded onto their computers. Each must also have microphones and speakers, and they had to log-on at the same time. When the connection was made, only one person could talk at a time, and the words were clipped, like talking on a radio. Fine for fun, but serious conversations were best suited to traditional telephones and telephone networks.

Many of the quality and functionality issues have been resolved. Big Business is looking at ways to use the Internet to at least augment its traditional communications networks and link its far-flung operations. Used right, international calling can be dirt-cheap—virtually free. While it's still in its infancy, and inexpensive, it will be worth your while to follow this topic closely. You can save a bundle of money if you make a lot of international calls.

E-mail: The Killer App

We haven't talked much about e-mail, but it's probably the single most important part of the Internet and electronic commerce, the "killer application," as industry experts like to call innovative uses for new technology. If you aren't using e-mail yet, you will be very soon. Remember back in the '80s those embarrassing times when someone would ask you for your fax number and you didn't have one yet? That's what's happening now with e-mail. The growing number of people who use e-mail everyday to communicate with co-workers, customers, vendors, and the world at large, are getting increasingly frustrated doing business with people who are not using e-mail. "It's so uncivilized and barbaric trying to communicate with people who don't have e-mail," says an e-mail user. "I hate it. I can never reach them and they can never reach me. We just keep playing tag until I contact someone else instead. I can't just sit around by my phone these days. They either do business the way I work, or I'll find someone else who will."

Not using e-mail is like not having voice mail or an answering machine. People simply can't reach you. This frustration is costing companies business. The question is not if you will be using e-mail as a core communications tool: it's only a question of when. So don't wait. If your customers use it, and your competitors use it, you'll use it, unless you have plans to close up shop. Customers are king, and they want to reach you the way *they* want to reach you, which makes it easy for them to do business with you.

E-mail is enthusiastically embraced by a growing number of people. It's also the only way to send a personal message to anyone, anytime, anywhere and have it arrive in minutes. It's easy to use, easy to learn, inexpensive, and it's becoming as much of a necessity as a fax, voice mail and a phone.

The Power of E-Mail and Electronic Messaging

Microsoft's home page has some interesting examples of how e-mail improves productivity and efficiency. Every person in business can relate to the mountain of "while-you-were-out" messages that pile up every time you go to lunch or to a meeting—or, even worse, on a business trip. Simply trying to keep up with messages on a timely basis is a big time-robber. According to Microsoft's home page, Peet's Coffee & Tea has turned e-mail into a big time-saver for its employees. Workers share detailed information inside the company, and with suppliers, vendors and customers outside the company, no matter when or where they are located.

Like voice mail, e-mail is an asynchronous form of communication. This means that the two parties don't have to coordinate schedules in order to communicate at the same time, as is the case with a phone conversation, which is known as synchronous communication. But e-mail is quick, accurate and informal, so several messages can be transmitted back and forth over the course of a day, accomplishing complex business transactions without ever talking on the phone, real-time, to the other party.

Like Fax-Back or Fax-on-Demand for E-mail

E-mail can be overwhelming. You can get hundreds, even thousands, of responses a day to an ad you've placed on the Internet, or to postings in various discussion groups. Rather than personally replying to each with the same information over and over, use technology to do the work. Use an auto-reply function from your e-mail provider. Once you have an Internet site, you can select more than one e-mail address for that site. Simply assign different addresses that will trigger different automatic replies. Basically an automatic form-letter response.

For instance, let's say you are placing ads around the Internet trying to get prospects to request more information on your product or service. Simply designate an e-mail box for this purpose and program it to auto-respond to any e-mail messages received, automatically sending out the desired information. This way, anyone can request information from you, 24 hours a day, and get it within minutes by simply sending you an e-mail message. You can designate several levels or different addresses for different information.

Auto-reply is great for customer service purposes, offering answers to frequently-asked questions. It is much like a fax-back or fax-on-demand service, using e-mail instead of faxes.

Solving Pre-Meeting Meetings

Fans of the immensely popular Dilbert cartoon might remember a piece on pre-meeting meetings, meetings, and post-meeting meetings, or debriefings. As funny as it sounds, planning meetings, actually having them, and wrapping up and summarizing the points of the meeting are essential, albeit often agonizing, steps in business life.

E-mail helps streamline—even eliminate—much of this real-time interaction by allowing participants to have a virtual meeting for all the functions that don't require face-to-face interaction. In many cases, this saves hours per day and allows participants to chime in and reply in *their* time frame, which allows them to do more in less time than ever before. No more sitting around a conference table for meetings that can be more easily handled with electronic messaging.

Document Sharing

Another benefit of e-mail is the ability to share documents. Employees at Peet's Coffee & Tea share pre-meeting documents via e-mail so that "people get to the meat of the issues much more quickly." Documents sent as attachments on compatible e-mail systems are viewable exactly as sent. That means you can distribute slide presentations, spreadsheets, graphics, word-processing documents, and more, and they will look exactly like the original printed version. Such information can be viewed on screen or printed out locally, or both.

This is how I submitted the manuscript for this book. I wrote the chapters, then saved them as a file. I then attached the file to an e-mail message and e-mailed it to my publisher, who received the file within minutes for editing directly on his computer.

In the old days, manuscripts were printed out and marked up. While this is still done, because all of my words are already keyed-in and on a computer disk, all the editor has to do is make the changes to the actual document on screen instead of having to retype the entire document. This edited file is then sent to the typesetter in digital form for actual graphical typesetting and design prior to printing. Because the manuscript stays in computer/digital form, it is easier than ever before to transmit, share, edit and manipulate. There is no longer any reason to key-in text more than once.

I also submit my columns to various publications through e-mail. Having everything in digital form streamlines the whole process. No more retyping entire articles and chapters. This streamlining has immeasurably improved the efficiency of the publishing business. These same benefits can impact your business communications.

Paperless Office

For years we've dreamed about the paperless office. Finally, it's coming true. As e-mail, voice mail, document sharing and other forms of electronic messaging catch on, we have less need for paper. "Paper just slows up the process," says one company owner.

Companies like VeriFone, a leader in the credit card verification business, have their employees linked electronically through these messaging technologies. Not only do they run the business on e-mail and groupware, but they also have virtually banned paper mail. How else could they efficiently hand-off work from group to group, completing projects in less time with less effort? Productivity increases while costs decrease.

What once was cutting-edge is becoming normal. If you are still buried under paper, you are not competitive. Believe me. Once you automate and link everyone electronically, you'll realize how sluggish your business had become.

Small businesses and home offices can get just as much value out of these services as large companies. Diane Gayeski, Ph.D.—a partner in OmniCom Associates, a consultancy specializing in organizational communications and learning systems—isn't new to this technology. Diane and her partner/husband have been using communications technology for 17 years. This has allowed them to live in Ithaca, N.Y., maintaining full-time faculty positions at Ithaca College, while working with large companies around the world.

"We use a whole range of technologies to do research, to collaborate with colleagues and clients all over the globe, and to mentor our clients as we co-design programs for them," says Gayeski. While they usually work from a home office, they regularly work with clients while "at the lake" via cellphone. They teach classes and work with students from Italy via e-mail, while managing a software project being developed by a programmer while he was on a six-month study trip to Japan. I get dizzy just thinking about all of this.

This is an excellent example of how new technologies can empower you to do things that simply aren't possible without them. The only limit is your imagination and creativity in devising ways to harness technology to solve your problems.

Work on Your Terms

E-mail and electronic messaging enable you to do work anytime, anyplace. Work from home, the airport, your hotel, a client's office, on vacation, anywhere.

I regularly work in several different places every day and have done so for years. With my laptop, cellular modem, cellphone and pager, I am never out of reach. I find the change of scenery does wonders for my outlook, refreshing my creativity.

In fact, as I write this, I am sitting in the front seat of my car, parked on a hilltop overlooking Atlanta. It's Springtime in Dixie, and the Dogwoods, Azaleas and assorted flowers have bloomed into an explosion of color and fragrance. Something you can't experience from an office cubicle.

This is what it's all about. Doing business on your terms. It's about freedom. About not being tied to the home or office. About cutting the cord and doing business where, when and how you want, while not missing a beat in the process.

Hire the Best People No Matter Where They Are

E-mail allows you to find and hire the best workers, no matter where they are located. I work with researchers, writers and editors scattered all over the country. Collaborating with e-mail and electronic messaging, we seldom need to meet face to face. This is the workplace of the future. Don't be tied to the traditional perceptions of a workplace. Unshackle yourself; break away from conventional thinking. There are so many creative and rewarding ways to do business and solve problems today, thanks to technology.

Say your business is based in Cleveland, and you are looking for a top-notch marketing manager. The best prospect, by far, happens to be located in San Diego, with no intention of moving east. Why not go ahead and hire her anyway? She can now telecommute, using all the latest communications technology, as if she were working in your Cleveland offices. Many businesses are hiring the best people they can find without regard to where they actually reside. More about this in Chapter 7.

Building Friendships With E-mail

In today's frantic business world, fewer than two in 10 telephone calls reach the intended party. Building relationships is getting more difficult all the time thanks to telephone tag. E-mail allows you to build relationships that might otherwise have died on the vine.

I talk with reporters on a daily basis. I've been talking with Kevin Maney for several years. Kevin is the technology reporter and columnist for *USA Today*, and author of *Megamedia Shakeout*. We share ideas and communicate back and forth via e-mail. Thanks to this efficient communications channel, we've gotten to know each other very well, without having ever met. At a recent *Communications Week* Networked Economy conference, I was a speaker and Kevin was there covering the event for *USA Today*. Despite the long odds, with some 500 attendees, we coincidentally sat down next to each other while one of the presentations was already in progress. It took 20 minutes or so for us to realize who we were sitting beside. Then, instantly, we both cracked big smiles burst into laughter. E-mail and electronic messaging had allowed us to develop a friendly relationship, and because of that there was an immediate bond when we finally met in person. The same thing happens with clients, associates, bosses, employees, and anyone else who matters to you.

E-mail revives the lost art of letter writing, yet it integrates the immediacy of the electronic age. It brings us the best of both worlds. It also serves as a handy permanent record of all communications. No more forgetting what was said on the phone a month ago. Just scroll through the outgoing messages, by date, recipient or subject, until you find the message in question.

It's Not What You Say But How You Say It

The only thing e-mail doesn't do very well is convey emotion. Like a letter, it's just text. Voice mail is better at this because you can convey enthusiasm, warmth or urgency with your tone of voice. To compensate, e-mail has developed funny little *emoticons*. These are symbols used to suggest a wide range of emotions. Like :-) for laughing or happy, and ;-) for winking, and all sorts of other imaginative combinations. Some people use them, others think they're silly. But at least they make it possible to convey some kind of emotion.

Audio/video e-mail is next. Like leaving a voice mail message, you'll soon be able to send an audio/video clip as an e-mail message. People will see you and hear your message. The technology is here already, though not yet widely used. This will become more widely accepted in coming years and eliminate the need for the silly emoticon symbols once and for all.

Get Closer to Your Customers

E-mail also allows small businesses, consultants or contract workers to work closely with larger client companies. If a larger company lives on e-mail and electronic messaging, you are out of the loop if you can't share and distribute information they way they do.

If they send and receive hundreds of e-mail messages a day and are used to getting lots of things done by simply hitting the reply button—answering questions and moving projects along—you have little chance of becoming synchronized with your clients and adding value to their work.

Management guru Tom Peters talks about the importance of getting close to your customers. Actually beyond close. He calls it *symbiosis*. Where you actually become so entwined with a customer's operation and processes that it's hard to tell where they leave off and you begin. This is an important concept for any business, large or small. To add value to your client's enterprise, you have to work the way they work. Increasingly, this means e-mail and electronic messaging. Faxes are great, but not enough. E-mail is where it's at.

Hygrade Distribution and Delivery Systems provides services such as warehousing and distributing furniture for retailers like

Federated Stores. Tom Higgerson, senior vice president for systems support, says, "We've hooked into Federated's e-mail system with terminals in our facilities. If we need to send out notification of special offers, and the buyer is traveling, it makes no difference where she is; we have near-instant access to her at any Federated location in the country. For both of us, e-mail is a fantastic communicator."

Hygrade has discovered the value of entwining systems with your customer. It is the wave of the future. *Someone* is going to be that close to your customers. Will it be you or your competitor?

Where to Sign Up for E-mail

E-mail comes in many flavors. On the high end, you can have your own e-mail domain name. Mine is *jeffkagan.com*. To send mail to me, you address it to *jeff@jeffkagan.com*. Contact an Internet service provider (ISP) to host your domain and let them do the work. ISPs can be smaller independent companies or the large local and long-distance phone companies, and anywhere in between. There are thousands from which to choose.

Ask the ISP if the domain name you want to register is available. If it isn't, think of another. If it is, reserve the name with the Internet naming authority. There is a charge for the name registration of about $200 for two years. Now that you have the name, set up your e-mail account with the ISP, which will provide access software and e-mail software to read, write and manage your e-mail messages. You'll pay the ISP a monthly fee to manage your domain and handle your e-mail, which runs from less than $10 per month to hundreds or even thousands of dollars if you are a large-volume user.

Another option is to simply sign up for e-mail with an e-mail service or online service. All the phone companies, as well as online services such as America OnLine, offer basic and advanced e-mail services. The cost can be very low; however, you don't have your own domain name. You have to use theirs.

A recent innovation is free e-mail. It's free to users, because the service sells advertising that accompanies each e-mail message. As long as you don't mind having an ad on each e-mail message, this is an affordable option. These services are typically less powerful than full-featured e-mail services, and they are more suitable for the casual user, as opposed to the more serious business user. However, if you want to check it out, such services are provided by Juno Online Services at *www.juno.com* and Freemark Communications at *www.freemark.com*. Freemark is also one of the firms offering permanent e-mail addresses, helping to solve the problem of changing addresses when you change services (see next section). Freemark users can choose from over 300 personalized domain names for their permanent e-mail address.

Incidentally, these free e-mail service providers offer a great illustration of entrepreneurs finding a niche, serving a market, starting a business and making money on the Net. Juno and Freemark have signed up hundreds of thousands of customers and many advertisers. Charles Ardai, president of Juno, told *Forbes*, "With all the exotic Internet uses, the humble e-mail is what people always come back to."

Changing E-mail Services

Unless you have your own e-mail domain name, you will have to change your e-mail address anytime you change your e-mail provider. This can be a real pain in the neck as e-mail becomes a more critical communications tool. The problem is that many e-mail providers do not offer a forwarding service if you switch providers. So you have to notify everyone on your e-mail directory of your new address.

If you do change providers, it's still a good idea to keep your old e-mail service active for at least six months, and to check it often to catch the folks who forgot to change your address or who never got the word in the first place. It's better than missing important messages.

Power and Peril of Instant Communications

Ever say something in the heat of the moment that you wish you could take back? That immediacy has a price: It's a double-edged sword. While e-mail doesn't appear to have the same hazards, since it's only notes appearing on your computer screen, don't be fooled. When replying to a regular letter, you take time to think about the subject, and carefully draft a reply. You then stamp it and drop it in the out-box. If you have second thoughts about what you have written, you only have to reach into the out-box and tear it up. Not with e-mail, which is immediate.

People who use e-mail regularly get lots of e-mail messages a day. They typically check mail several times a day, download whatever is there at the time, read and reply to them on the spot, and then go back to work. This is fine for routine correspondence or inquiries; however, be very careful about what you say in your haste to clean out your in-box.

E-mail is Forever

Just because you can send a reply to an e-mail message instantly doesn't mean you should. Unlike regular mail, e-mail is easy to reply to; all you have to do is hit the *reply* icon. Every e-mail user occasionally regrets sending a reply or message too hastily. The immediacy can catch you off-guard. You really have to consider e-mail the near equivalent of having a face-to-face conversation.

Don't merely be careful what you say; be careful about how you say it. Humor and sarcasm do not translate easily in e-mail text. What you may mean in good humor can be taken the wrong way by the reader, which can create hard feelings and strained relationships.

Not only that, but e-mail is forever. It's almost too easy to send and reply to e-mail. That's what makes it a powerful tool. However, like using any power tool, you've got to use it with respect. E-mail resides on e-mail servers, computers with huge hard-drives. Every message ever sent on any e-mail system anywhere is archived somewhere and can be pulled up at any time. Recent news stories tell of companies being sued for discrimination because of e-mailed "harmless" jokes relating to race or sex, or some other politically incorrect topic of the day. E-mail messages can also be subpoenaed by the court in lawsuits.

Not only does e-mail stay around in cyberspace forever, it also can be forwarded to others with push of a button. This is how documents and messages are sent to numerous employees in an organization. This is also how some of those "harmless" jokes are forwarded throughout the company. So don't say anything in e-mail you wouldn't say in person or in a letter. Don't say anything you wouldn't want passed around. If something is very sensitive, or could be taken the wrong way, a personal telephone call is still the best bet. As powerful and valuable as it is, if used inappropriately, e-mail can be embarrassing and costly. E-mail is by no means private.

E-mail Saves Money

E-mail cuts phone bills. The average telephone call lasts a bit more than three minutes, which is where long-distance bills add up. But e-mail is virtually free. Pay your flat monthly bill and unlimited e-mail comes with it in most cases. This is an oversimplification, but the point is valid. Electronic messaging is cheaper than phone calls. Even voice mail, averaging a minute a message, is cheaper than phone conversations.

Invasion of Privacy

Many employees are shocked to discover that their employers can and do monitor their voice mail and e-mail. The very nature of these communications methods lulls you into believing they are private. This is not the case, and the law is in favor of the employer. Since employers pay for the technology, it's a business tool, and they own it. They have the right to monitor or use it however they want. Companies often warn users and customers that they may be monitored for the sake of training or customer service. Either way, whether they warn you or not, always assume that e-mail and voice mail are not private. Never say anything you wouldn't want your boss to read or hear.

Online Goldmine

There are so many valuable services and so much powerful information online. For example, I regularly book my travel plans online. I scan the flights using the same service the travel agents use. Direct connections are available, or you can gain access through many commercial online services like Microsoft Network, CompuServe, America Online and Prodigy.

When you are traveling and you accidentally delete files from your laptop, how do you get them back? Your backup discs or tapes are back at the office or at home. Well, all is not lost. New services allow you to back up your hard-drive over phone lines or over the Internet, instead of using your floppies or tape backup system. This way, you can access your backed-up data at any time from wherever you are located. McAfee Associates, the anti-virus people, offer WebStor. Another is SUREFIND, which is available online. Atrieva Internet Backup makes scheduled connections to your ISP, backs up changed or new files, and scans all files for viruses.

There are also automobile buying services online, such as Auto-By-Tel and Auto Advantage, as well as many individual dealers and car buying/selling services. AutoConnect, another buying source, has signed up 4,000 dealerships and is one of the largest auto industry Internet sites.

Edmunds Car Guides is online, along with many others, listing the value of automobiles in which you are interested. So is *Consumer Reports*, with its auto-buying information. In fact, hundreds of auto-related services are online, which puts the power in the consumer's hand when buying a car.

Online services like Compuserve, AOL, and Microsoft Network—plus individual company Web pages and government sites on the Internet—offer a wide range of small business resources. I guarantee that if you spend some time and dip your ladle into the torrential river of information online, you'll find more valuable answers and loads of pertinent competitive and business information than you would have ever imagined.

Various phone company Internet home pages are an incredible wealth of information for operating and growing small businesses. It's a virtual goldmine. It'll take some time to find what you want, and you'll end up with mountains more than you ever thought you needed, but once you get to know the search engines, you can usually find what you want quickly. The only problem is pulling yourself away, because the Internet can be even more engaging than thumbing your way through a set of colorful encyclopedias used to be. You just never know what interesting piece of information or site you are going to uncover next.

Internet Faxing

When technologies blend, problems get solved. Case in point: New fax services use the Internet. Go to any search engine, and enter *Internet Faxing*, and many such services will be listed. These new services demonstrate how new businesses are being made possible by the Internet and new technologies. The service itself works in a variety of ways.

In essence, you send a fax to a fax service on the Internet or to your ISP. Increasingly, ISPs are offering Internet faxing services. The fax is routed in digital form (which is what faxes are) over the Internet, instead of over long-distance lines, to the destination city. By avoiding long-distance charges, even international faxes can theoretically be sent for the cost of a local call. Of course the fax service charges a fee to send the fax, but that cost is only a fraction of what an international long-distance fax call would be. If you send lots of long-distance faxes, especially international faxes, this is something to consider.

Blending the Internet with Telemarketing

Another technology blend combines the power of telemarketing, or the call center, with the Internet. For the last 30 years or so, 800 numbers have played an increasingly important role in commerce. However, the Internet is also growing in importance for sales and service. Elizabeth Stites of Matrixx Marketing told *Communications Week*, "The explosive growth of the Internet is being compared to the introduction of 800 numbers 25 years ago as a way of communicating more effectively with customers."

Many computer companies have only online customer service operations. While this is not welcomed by customers who want to talk to someone live, it is a blessing for customers who want answers to frequently-asked questions after hours.

Some of the larger local and long-distance phone companies have begun integrating their Internet and call-center technologies. This allows business customers that use both technologies to link them together. For example, when a customer of yours is shopping on the Net and finds your home page, he will also see a button he can click with the mouse, alerting one of your telemarketing call-center operators to call him. A live conversation is then be conducted while the customer is viewing your Web page. Your call-center operator can also place additional information onto the customer's screen to help the him make a purchase decision.

We are going to see more of this interaction between the telephony network and the Internet networks. This blending is going to be a key trend. Telephone companies are weaving the Internet into their telephony strategies and, before long, the two will be seamlessly interwoven and work smoothly together. This has powerful implications for marketing online. This multimedia electronic commerce experience will change the way we shop, buy and sell.

The Power of Traditional Telemarketing

With all this talk of new technologies, I must at least mention the power of traditional telemarketing. All those sales calls you get at the office (business to business) and at home (business to consumer) continue for a reason. They work.

MCI, the biggest telemarketer in the country, has built its business in large part through the power of telemarketing and call-center technology—the same services you can use to build *your* business. Remember, MCI didn't start out as an $18 billion dollar corporation and the nation's second-largest long-distance company. It started out with only a handful of employees and a dream to be much more. Telemarketing was an important factor in its success.

So, Can You Make Money on the Internet?

I hope it is becoming clear that the Internet, e-mail and all the varieties of electronic commerce are not a passing fad. Not even a trend. But the wave of the future. And the future is not some far-off point. It's here and now.

Don't worry if all this seems a bit overwhelming. Everyone is in the same boat. This is the time to be playing around and experimenting to find what works, what doesn't, and why. Go ahead and make mistakes. Now is the time. Customers are experimenting with new ways of shopping. Don't make the mistake of assuming today's customer isn't yet ready to embrace electronic commerce because it's too confusing and clunky to survive. Customers will get increasingly used to shopping and doing business this way. It puts the power in their hands. Customers who are skeptical today about electronic commerce will likely be quite comfortable with it a year from now. Some sooner, others later, but it's just around the corner.

Chapter 7
Telecommuting and
Workplace Alternatives

Atlanta's Great
Olympic Telecommuting Experiment

According to *USA Today*, commuters in one-third of the nation's largest cities annually spend an entire workweek stuck in traffic jams. Researchers using 1993 data (the most recent available) peg the cost of this gridlock in the top 50 cities at $51 billion. What a waste!

Atlanta's 1996 Olympic summer was dubbed the "Great Telecommuting Experiment." Not only did Atlanta welcome the world to the Centennial Olympic Games, but the business community also had the unique opportunity to test its telecommuting capabilities.

What did Atlanta businesses learn from this experience? Most Atlanta businesses delayed any significant changes from business-as-usual until the Olympics were just weeks away. They braced for Olympic-related traffic gridlock by scrambling to set up telecommuting programs and business-continuity plans, which would allow their people to work through those three magical weeks of summer games. Now that the dust has settled, it's time to take a look at what worked, what didn't, and why.

I was the lunch speaker at an annual telecommuting conference in Atlanta that focused on this topic. "One Stop Telecommuting," the Fifth Annual Southeastern Telecommuting Conference, hosted by the non-profit Metro Atlanta Telecommuting Advisory Council (MATAC), brought together industry experts, vendors and executives responsible for telecommuting programs in their companies.

"Companies across Atlanta got their feet wet testing telecommuting," said telecommuting consultant Michael Dziak, president of InteleWorks and general manager of MATAC. "It was a taste of things to come, and most were pleased with the results."

While telecommuting is still far from mainstream, those who are embracing it find many benefits. The consensus is that companies and workers that were already using telecommuting and alternative workplace programs didn't miss a beat during the Olympics. Those that rushed to set up programs at the last minute, or that didn't do anything at all, didn't see any benefit. Those unlucky businesses caught within the Olympic "circle" wound up taking three-week vacations or getting to work at 6 a.m. and leaving after 9 p.m. to avoid traffic.

The biggest issues surrounding telecommuting don't seem to revolve around the technology, although that's obviously a big part. Instead, the big obstacles are the soft issues, the people issues, and the politics of telecommuting. Getting top management and the workers themselves to buy-into the idea. And buying-in is critical for success in coming years.

Managers worry about the cost of the technology and the loss of direct, line-of-sight control over worker productivity. This is really more of a management problem than anything else, and the way employee performance is measured can and will change. The other side of the coin are the telecommuters themselves. They have to deal with all the challenges and benefits that come with working at home, or from an alternate work site. Issues like family distractions, loss of colleague contact and interaction, and forgetting where the off-button is located, are just a few of the factors new telecommuters have to deal with. They need to develop a whole new group of skills and work habits.

The benefits can be very inviting, however. Happier employees getting more work done in less time without the constant and annoying office distractions, phone calls, and meetings. More time with the family, avoiding the rush-hour crunch, and generally enjoying a better quality of life.

The people issues that need to be worked out boil down to changing the way we think about work. "Increasingly, work is no longer a place we go, but a thing we do," says Gil Gordon of Gil Gordon Associates, a Monmouth Junction, New Jersey-based telecommuting consulting firm. The dynamics of the work force are changing, and companies that don't change along with them will find themselves at a competitive disadvantage.

The best workers will migrate to companies with the most flexible work environment. Increasingly, as technology allows workers to do their jobs anywhere, more will be choosing to work from home offices. This blending of work and play, home and office, are going to become more entrenched in our work-life culture.

Teleworking also helps to resolve the conflict between stay-at-home and career parents. It allows parents to spend more time at home with the family, and get more work done simultaneously. This not only improves quality-of-life issues for workers, but it also breeds loyalty to the organization. Such employees work harder and stay with the company longer, because they know a good thing when they see it.

Companies that are proactive in creating a workplace around worker preferences will be rewarded with the best and most loyal employees. Teleworking is becoming a powerful way to recruit top talent from all over the country, even all over the world. Thanks to faxes, e-mail, groupware, audio and video conferencing, and all the other technologies we've discussed, it's as easy to work with someone across the country as it is with someone across the street. Allowing top talent to choose their home base is a powerful enticement.

Teleworking is also a great way to prepare for seasonal or cyclical business swings. As your business activity increases and decreases, you can quickly gear up or throttle back as needed with a pool of teleworking talent. Businesses already using temporary seasonal workers or freelancers have found that this makes sense and saves money.

Forward-thinking companies are moving away from traditional office space and moving toward virtual office space. Inside the office, this means "hoteling." Instead of each person being assigned a permanent desk, the workplace is a well-thought-out maze of generic cubicles and desks. You own your computer and your cart, which you can wheel to any available desk. This allows teams to quickly form, find a place together to tackle projects, then quickly disband and move on without missing a beat.

Hoteling also means creating alternative workplaces away from the traditional office. Satellite offices are a good example. You can set up several smaller offices equipped with faxes, printers, computers, modems, and so on, which is perfect for a mobile sales force. The average employee occupies his office desk only one-third of the time. That means expensive office space, leased at rates as high as $50 per square foot annually, is unused two-thirds of the time. Corporate America simply can't tolerate this kind of waste and expect to stay competitive.

Such portable technologies as laptop computers, modems, e-mail, wireless modems, the Internet and intranets also allow your workers to work at a customer's office, or from on the road. They can be as productive as if they were sitting at their regular office desk.

Send Your People Home to Work

John Keller, telecom reporter for the *Wall Street Journal*, installed a second phone line in his home so he could go home to get more work done. "I find that sometimes I just have to get away from the office, the ringing phones, and the other demands and distractions, just to be able to focus on an important article." Keller uses his second phone line to interview experts and newsmakers, and to log on with his computer and connect to the office. That way, he can file his stories via a modem from the solitude of his home office. "Sometimes I get more work done in my home office, in a few hours with no distractions, than I can get done in a whole day at the office. Not to mention the avoided commute time."

Environmental issues are also driving the move to telecommuting. The fewer people tied up in rush-hour traffic, the better it is for the environment, because air pollution is reduced. Atlanta has been struggling with clean-air issues for years, and getting more cars off the road is a great help. During the Olympics, "Atlanta was in a traffic petri dish of sorts," said Ed Ellis, president of LRE Engineering, Inc., who has been analyzing traffic and transportation trends around Atlanta for over 24 years. In an *Atlanta Business Chronicle* article, Ellis said, "Overall, Atlanta did well during the Olympic Games. My sincere hope is that this was a view of what will be and not merely a teaser of what could have been."

A side benefit of sending some folks home to work is a reduction in office-space requirements, which can mean significant savings to the bottom line. While these cost savings are what first piques the curiosity of corporate execs, increased productivity and a happier, more stable work force are even more important to the future of their businesses.

"If telecommuting is a real focus, and companies prepare their employees both psychologically and with technology, it can be the most productivity-enhancing thing a company can do," says June Langhoff, author of *The Telecommuters Advisor* (Aegis, 1996). "As with anything else, if done right, it can be great. If done wrong, it can be a big flop, and even a drain."

According to *Communications Week*, Georgia Power makes telecommuting look easy. The utility company uses a nine-step checklist for ensuring telecommuting success:

1. Get an executive to champion the program so it gets the resources it needs.
2. A multidisciplinary task force ensures the input and guidance of multiple constituencies.
3. Objectives must be measurable.
4. Policies and procedures should be clear.
5. Match participants to the demands and responsibilities of telecommuting (it isn't for everyone).
6. Make sure the budget is adequate.
7. Procure the right services, equipment and support.
8. Training is critical.
9. Be willing to make adjustments to incorporate the benefit of experience and changing business conditions.

So where do you turn for assistance in getting set up? Be aware that this is not a place to be poking around in the dark. Talk with people who understand the technologies that are available, and who can understand your business needs—and who know how to merge the two harmoniously. Local and long-distance telephone companies are a good place to start. While the services they offer are not new, the concept of bundling them together in the right combinations helps to enable a successful telecommuting workforce.

A good source of information is available on the Internet. Check out Gil Gordon's Web site at *www.gilgordon.com* for some good ideas. Gordon also puts on an annual telecommuting conference, which is a good source of information and up-to-date strategies. Gordon has developed telecommuting and alternative workplace programs to help you ease into this new way of doing business. Another good site is that of author June Langhoff, at *www.infographex.com/langhoff*. She has wriiten several books on the topic.

This is an important trend to prepare for. You don't want to be late to this dance, because if you are, the best workers will have gone to your competition, leaving you with the leftovers. That's not the right stuff for gaining competitive advantage.

Although telecommuting might be taking awhile to be widely accepted and integrated into mainstream corporate life, one thing is clear. Those using it now are realizing significant competitive advantages. They are positioning themselves to be the leaders when the rest of the world finally catches on and scrambles to set up telecommuting programs. Just like those Atlanta businesses that waited until only a few weeks before the Olympics. Have you thought about sending your employees home to work? Maybe now is a good time to consider a telecommuting program.

Tips for Road Warriors: Don't Touch that Phone!

Working on the road is a form of telecommuting, and here are some tips that will save you money on your next business trip. Most business travelers are overcharged for telephone calls when staying at hotels. In fact, the unwary traveler who needs to make many calls can spend as much on the hotel phone bill as the room itself. Hotels see their telephone systems as profit centers, and add surcharges and premiums everywhere they can. That doesn't mean that you have to get caught in every money-gobbling trap they set. Here are a few money-saving tips to arm yourself with next time you hit the road.

First of all, NEVER use the hotel's long-distance service. It often inflates the cost of the call by adding hefty surcharges and premiums. The cost of a long-distance call on a hotel system can be several times more expensive than using your own service.

The least expensive way to call the office is to use your company's 800 number. The rates are often 20 cents per minute, or less, and no surcharges will be assessed. Compare that to a hotel surcharge of 50 cents to $1.50 per call, and a 40% (or more) premium tacked on to every minute.

If you travel often, consider a Personal 800 Number, now being offered by a few long-distance carriers. Like business 800 numbers, the rates are low and there are no surcharges per call. You can even give this 800 number to your kids at college, or to grandma and grandpa, who might not otherwise call as often because they can't afford to.

When you call someplace other than your home or office, use either your long-distance calling card, or one of the new prepaid debit cards (also called *prepaid phone cards* and *telecards*). Your calling card usually has a surcharge, but it is often less than that of the hotel, and the per-minute rate is usually substantially less than that charged by the hotel. The prepaid debit card avoids all hotel charges because you dial a toll-free 800 number first, to get into the computerized system, before dialing the number you wish to call.

Prepaid debit cards are also a great way to call from the road. They are similar to calling cards, except they come in prepaid denominations (usually $5-$50). They are also great for giving to employees because they limit your liability to the amount on the face of the card.

Even though the hotel might not use the same long-distance carrier as yours, by law it must allow you to connect to your own long distance service. The law requires hotels to post instructions on how to reach your carrier. If you do not find such instructions by the phone, call the hotel operator and ask to be connected. It's worth the effort. Often, the hotels that make it the most difficult to bypass their expensive system are the ones that charge the highest rates. If you think a hotel is playing games, and intentionally making it too difficult to reach your carrier, report them to the FCC.

If you make several long distance calls, one after the other, here's another tip. Don't hang up between calls. Press the pound key (#) instead. This will give you another dial tone from your long distance-calling card, without hanging up first. Not only does this save time and aggravation of dialing your ridiculously long calling-card codes, but it also eliminates an additional surcharge from the hotel for each call. If you make 10 calls, paying one surcharge of $1 for all of them, rather that the $1 surcharge for each call... well you can see the point here.

Also remember to keep a log of every call you make. Note whether it was completed or not. Then compare this log to the bill at checkout time. In most instances you will find you are being charged for calls that were never completed, calls that reached a busy signal, or calls that never answered. That's because hotels often charge for each attempt, whether or not the call was completed. They often begin charging after a certain number of seconds. Challenge the calls you didn't make. The desk clerk will usually remove them from the bill.

Phone systems are one of the big profit centers for hotels, right along with room rates and food service. Now you know how to bypass some of these traps, and avoid being overcharged while on the road. If, like the average business traveler, you make plenty of calls from your room to stay in touch, these tips can easily cut your hotel bills by 10-20%.

Free cellular phones, which come with many rental cars, are also a source of expense-account overload. The lure of a handy phone quickly turns into a nightmare when phone charges amounting to hundreds of dollars get tacked onto the rental bill. This happened to publisher Virginia Knott. She told *USA Today* that she rented a phone from the rental car agency when she forgot to pack her own cellphone. She made 1,100 minutes worth of calls and got a bill for a whopping $2,345! Granted, this is more minutes than the average user would rack up, however, at roughly $2 per minute, how long would it take you to say *ouch*?

The same with airphones, those handy airplane phones that are conveniently located within arm's reach on the seatback in front of you. Prices will continue to vary as the providers experiment with flat fees and per-minute charges, until they finally settle on a model that works. Any way you slice it, however, these calls will remain expensive for quite a while. They have their place. They are convenient and valuable, but expensive. Enough said.

Chapter 8
Putting All
the Pieces Together

Cutting Through the Fog of Confusion:
Separating Hype From Reality

Where Do We Go From Here?

Recently, I stumbled across a painting titled *A Nation in Transition*, a nighttime city scene at the turn of the century. On one side of the bustling city street was a horse and buggy going away; on the other side, an early automobile coming forward. One side of the busy street was lit by gas lanterns, while the other was illuminated by electric lights. People were hustling and bustling about, and you got a real sense of the turmoil society was going through during the transition from an agricultural to an industrial society. The automobile, the telephone, radio, and a whole litany of new inventions were changing the way we lived and worked, which transformed our economy and our entire society.

A hundred years later, we're going through another transition of historic proportions—a communications and information revolution with as significant an impact on our lives. We are evolving from an analog world based on tangible matter to a digital world based on the byte, information and knowledge. The same types of people and companies that succeeded during the last revolution will be the same types that thrive during this one. Those who recognize and embrace the unstoppable march of change and who look for new opportunities created by the resulting chaos.

The way we do business and create wealth are changing. Instant access to information and anytime/anyplace communications are changing the rules for success. More twenty-something millionaires, even billionaires, who are tuned into the changes that are rocking our world. Think of names like Yahoo, Netscape, and the growing list of successful software and technology companies. These companies rocketed into the limelight and made fortunes for their founders in a few short years. Think these were the last? On the contrary, there are only the beginning. Small businesses and entrepreneurs have a front-row seat for the wild ride on which we have just embarked as a society, and the biggest breakthroughs and overnight fortunes are going to come from them.

At the very least, today's communications technologies can improve what you already do. For example, busy restaurants give pagers to their customers and beep them when their table is ready. Patrons are not forced to sit tethered to the restaurant bar, and are free to stroll nearby until they are paged, which gives these restaurants a significant edge over their competitors. However, individuals and companies must avoid thinking in terms of incremental improvements in today's products and services. Instead, we must think in terms of a quantum leap. We have to look at today's problems, challenges and opportunities and invent totally new ways of solving and profiting from them.

This is truly a golden age we are entering. An age of incredible wealth creation. And today's leaders aren't guaranteed to be tomorrow's leaders. The biggest companies are struggling with their sheer size at a time when they need to act small so they too, can be nimble and entrepreneurial. What used to be their strength—size and numbers of customers—is today slowing them down.

Sure, times are confusing, but this is not the time to be frozen in the headlights. Now is the time to boldly go where we've never gone before. We haven't seen this much opportunity and challenge in our entire lifetimes. And small businesses in particular have the opportunity to strike it big, and play by their own rules. So go out and stake your claim. Make one of your million-dollar ideas pay off. Somebody's going to, it might just as well be you!

Customer Intimacy is Key

In his book *Customer Intimacy*, Fred Wiersema talks about transcending simply getting close to the customer; he talks about getting intimate with the customer. About building close, win-win relationships with customers. Beyond strong working relationships. Beyond good business relationships, toward customer-intimate relationships. If that's an important goal, and I think it is, then today's technology empowers you to be there for your customers and to build those relationships.

Providing World-Class Service is Key

Do you think U.S. businesses provide world-class service and goods? Well, they are better than the goods and services produced by many other countries, but there's plenty of room for improvement. And there are plenty of home-grown companies just waiting for their competitors to falter. This presents a strategic opportunity for entrepreneurs who grasp the concept.

Here is a partial list of some underlying deficiencies that create unique competitive opportunities, compiled by the International Customer Service Association:

❏ 5,517,200 cases of soft drinks produced in the next 12 months will be flat.

❏ 2,488,200 books will be shipped in the next year with the wrong cover.

❏ 2 million documents will be lost by the IRS this year.

❏ 268,500 defective tires will be shipped this year.

❏ 114,500 mismatched pairs of shoes will be shipped this year.

❏ 22,000 checks will be deducted from the wrong bank accounts in the next 60 minutes.

❏ 18,322 pieces of mail will be mishandled in the next hour.

❏ 3,506 copies of tomorrow's *Wall Street Journal* will be missing one of the three sections.

❏ 1,314 phone calls will be misplaced by telecommunications services in the next minute.

❏ 12 babies will be given to the wrong parents today.

You get the point. Companies that focus on offering world-class service have the edge; technology can make the difference.

The Virtual CEO

Technology allows you to run your business from anywhere. This has not always been the case. After building a successful company, business people had to stay in close proximity to stay on top of things; they were bound by their success. Increasingly, entrepreneurs are heading for the places others only dream about, and are running their businesses remotely.

Bob Sommers, CEO of Sommers Communication, built a business providing customer-service training for large companies and organizations. After years of hard work and struggle, he landed several large contracts, which set the company on a success track others only dream about. Sommers packed up his family and moved to Hawaii, where he keeps in touch with his office thanks to the technologies we've discussed. He lives the dream most of us only fantasize about.

This technology enables and empowers you to take on the world on your terms. You can write your own rules and enjoy life as never before. You no longer need to be a slave to your business. Sure, if abused, technology can be a real pain in the neck. Some people just can't unhook and lead a normal existence. But if you know where the *Off* button is and how to use it, the technology can give you the control and freedom you seek.

The Virtual Company

Many companies are either changing their processes or starting from scratch to take advantage of the technology revolution. In a *Business Week* story about Rickard Associates, it was revealed that the only three people who show up for work at the office are Wendy Rickard, her assistant and a part-time employee. The rest of the staff is scattered around the country. An art director in Arizona. A few editors in Florida, Georgia, Michigan and Washington, D.C., as well as loads of freelance workers scattered all over. This is a great example of how businesses are breaking the rules and taking advantage of opportunities created by technology.

Don't Sit This One Out

Just because you may not understand all the new communications technologies and choose not to implement them, don't make the mistake of assuming your competition is doing the same. That assumption could quickly put you at a measurable disadvantage. Most of us didn't grow up with technology the way our children have. We don't feel as comfortable with it as the next generation does. In fact, many of us have an inherent bias against technology, which can hinder us in business. A bias that our competitors may not have, especially when you consider that we are emerging into the global marketplace, and the fresh crop of young workers and managers are quite comfortable with technology.

Just as important, many of our home-grown entrepreneurs are more willing to use *all* the technology at their disposal to break into your industry and to earn market share. You must stay on the cutting edge yourself.

Frozen in the Headlights

Don't let the confusion prevent you from jumping in and using these new tools. A recent study by MCI shows that three of five Americans describe themselves as "resistant to" or "hesitant about" communications technologies. The study, conducted by MCI One with clinical psychologist Michelle M. Weil, Ph.D., found that 59% of respondents describe their attitudes toward technology as "hesitant, prove it" or "resistant and frustrated." Only 35% consider themselves "first in line" in their attitudes about technology.

Despite the technophobia, 39% of non-technology users say they will be using these technologies by the year 2000. They realize that they will have to come aboard, kicking and screaming, at some point in the near future. The question is, will you be leading the pack or playing catch up? *When* you jump on board plays a big part in that outcome. The longer you wait, the more costly it will be.

Big Companies are Afraid of You

I am continually amazed when business leaders tell me that one of their biggest competitive worries is an upstart, coming out of no where, with a breakthrough idea to challenge their market position. Most larger companies are increasingly afraid of being one-upped by smaller, entrepreneurial competitors that are more nimble, reactive and quickly able to sense and respond to subtle market changes. I call this the elephant-and-the-mouse syndrome. Take advantage of your small size; don't ignore its benefits.

Price of Entry is Dropping

Thanks to technology, it is easier and less expensive for a start-up to get into business and become your competitor than it was for you when you started. In fact, if you had to start your business today, it would most likely be substantially different from it's current form, because you would not be hindered by old ideas and preconceived notions. It is important to stay on the cutting edge of technology to retain your edge. Your competitors are. On the other hand, the same thing that makes is easier for start-ups to compete with you, also makes it easier for you to compete with your larger competitors.

New competitors are redefining the rules of every industry. That's why larger companies watch smaller companies so closely. Not because they pose an immediate competitive threat, but because they want to know what their new competitors are offering customers that is over and above traditionally-accepted standards of service. Service they will have to start providing themselves or risk losing business. That watermark of service keeps rising, and the impetus often comes from small, innovative businesses and new competitors.

Anywhere/Anytime Communications

Nearly 45 million cellular phones are in use in the United States today; roughly half of the households in America. That's a lot of phones, and they're just scratching the surface. There are almost as many pagers clipped to the belts of Americans. In the next few years it's projected that 100 million of us will have cellphones and pagers.

As more wireless competition moves in, prices will drop, fueling more people to sign up. Companies that use these services today still have an edge. Before long, these will be standard business tools.

These People are Your Customers

The ability to never be out of touch is not only effective, it is also quickly becoming mandatory. Most people and businesses are moving so fast they need to stay in touch with each other and their offices. These people become accustomed to instant access and fewer roadblocks, which can be addictive. Impediments become frustrating and unacceptable. These people are also customers. Your customers. If you are not always available to them, they will find someone who is.

Going the Way of the Buggy Whip Industry

Since it is more cost-effective and infinitely preferable to retain an existing customer, rather than replacing him with a new one, the answer is obvious. Embrace all the new emerging technologies and communications tools that will help keep your customers happy. It can cost hundreds of dollars, even thousands, to land one new customer, by the time you add up all the advertising costs, sales staff salaries and overhead that goes into the effort. It makes sense to do everything you can to protect that investment by hanging on to every precious customer as if he is worth his weight in gold. Those who do not only will survive, but thrive in coming years. Those who don't will go the way of the buggy whip industry and fade into obscurity.

Accelerated Pace of Change

Change used to take a decade or more. Look at how long it took cellular phones to catch on. It took 10 years from 1983 to 1993 to reach the first 10 million phones. It's only taken the next three years, to 1996, to quadruple that number to more than 40 million phones.

Fax machines caught on even more quickly. Now e-mail is on fire, having taken only a few years to become a core and vital business communications tool for millions of businesses in America. Video conferencing is next. And so much of the way we communicate and do business will play itself out or be enabled by the evolving Internet.

We no longer have years to get used to change; we have to be sensitive to change and act quickly. "Sensing and responding will replace making and selling, and companies that successfully manage a product through its entire life cycle will emerge the market leaders," said Anderson Consulting partner Carleton F. Kilmer in an *Industry Week* article. The old adage, "Hesitate and you are lost" needs to be updated to the '90s version, "Delay and you're dust."

Not If, But When

Many entrepreneurs are too busy running their own businesses to think about adopting new technologies. They hope it's a fad and will go away. This is the biggest mistake a business can make. That's what the buggy whip makers said.

Well, you couldn't stop this information, communications and technology revolution if you tried. So why fight it. Leverage it. Look for the new opportunities and pounce on them before your competitors do. You really have little choice. You can either embrace these changes now or play catch up later. You might say you won't be using e-mail and video conferencing, but if your customers prefer it and your competitors use it, well… it's not a question of *if* any longer. It's only a question of *when* you will get with the program. And the longer you wait, the further behind you will be, and the more it will cost you in lost business to get up to speed.

Intimidating? Yes!

But don't let this stop you from using these resources. The biggest mistake you can make is assuming that your competition is not moving ahead with this. They are looking for that edge, too. With all the changes going on in the industry, it's only getting more confusing. One-stop shopping will be one of the biggest trends in coming years. Buying all your communications and information services from one company. Having your local and long-distance phone service, paging, cellular, e-mail, video conferencing, news and information, Internet access, electronic commerce, and all the other services which are coming down the pike—all on one account and on one bill.

And that way, you'll have lower costs due to the volume discounts they'll all count toward. One 800 number to call if you have questions or need service. One company to deal with instead of a handful. Life will be much less complicated when you can choose one company you trust to handle it all. A friend in the communications business. There's still no such thing as a complete one-stop shop, but companies are working toward that goal. Phone companies are becoming more than just phone companies. Just look at the variety of products and services they offer these days. They are evolving into diversified communications enterprises.

Things are moving faster than ever before, and there are going to be more changes in the next few years than we've seen in our entire lifetimes. Learn to love change, or at least get comfortable about it. Look for all the new opportunities hiding just beneath the surface. Embrace all the new technologies and tools that can help you do more business and gain an edge over your competitors.

In coming years, these tools will be widely used by everyone, just like the fax machine. They'll simply be core communications tools. The cost of doing business. Don't get paralyzed by that "frozen in the headlights" mentality. Now is the time to start exploring with all these new tools. When it's okay to make mistakes. Barry Bonds, the highest-paid baseball player in the United States, says, "I get paid millions of dollars a year to fail 70% of the time." The same applies to you. There are no hard-and-fast rules.

Experiment, and feel free to make mistakes, because that's how you'll learn what works. Your customers are expecting you to make mistakes today. Everyone else is. A few years from now, it'll be too late. By then, your customers will expect you to know what you are doing—and they won't be so forgiving.

Don't miss this opportunity to experiment and figure out what works in your business. This is not a time to be shy or timid. The way we do business is changing, and it pays to be a leader. As Lee Iacocca used to say in those Chrysler commercials, "Either lead, follow or get out of the way." Well, in the communications revolution, if you don't lead you might get lost among the laggards.

Automate or Become Irrelevant

One of the smartest things you can do is arm yourself and your people with laptops, cellphones, pagers, e-mail, Internet access and all the other communication tools for doing business today. Richard Feldstein, CEO of Aspen Press, Ltd., a children's book publisher, told *Business Week* that Aspen receives orders and payments electronically from large retailers. Without the electronic link, Feldstein said, his company might be out of the loop. His larger retailer customers are paring down their supplier lists and eliminating companies that are behind the technology curve. Feldstein added that those who don't embrace these technologies are usually the first to go.

Bye-Bye Middle Man

A more profound impact on business will be the demise of the middle man. Technology will replace the need for traditional travel agents who don't find ways to create value for customers beyond printing tickets. All of those people and businesses that stand between the product source and the ultimate consumer are becoming superfluous. With electronic commerce, we don't need them as much anymore to help us get what we need. If you are a middleman business, find ways to add value or find something else to do.

Erasing Time, Space and Geographic Restraints

Technology is changing the social fabric of our world. It's also erasing the restrictions time, space and geography. People can do business anywhere/anytime/anyplace, hiring the best and working for the best companies.

Technology is also a solution to some welfare issues. It allows workers to find gainful employment without geographic constraints. It also allows disabled workers to rejoin the work force. The same telecommuting and alternative workplace solutions enable us to fix many of our social and welfare problems, bringing millions of Americans back into the workforce to be productive once again.

Perpetual Change and Perpetual Learning

The pace of change is frantic. The sheer magnitude of constant change is mind-boggling. The only solution is perpetual learning. There is no such thing as treading water; you are either swimming ahead or sinking. It takes constant effort and perpetual learning to forge ahead, which is today's reality, and the formula for success.

You've got to be an opportunist, with your radar up and your ear to the ground every day. This is a time of historic and profound change. This isn't a short-term fad. This is a permanent shift in the way we do things. Ignore this fact at your own risk. In a few years, your business will either be floundering or flourishing, depending upon your grasp of the communications and information revolution, the steps you take today, and your ability to leverage the forces that are changing the way business is done.

Tell Me Your Stories

I get my best ideas from business people just like you. People who experiment and try new things with technology to find solutions to business problems. I'd love to hear your stories. The good, the bad, the ugly, the cool, the amazing, the embarrassing, and the funny.

Write to me at jeff@jeffkagan.com, or send regular mail to:

Jeffrey Kagan
P.O. Box 670562
Marietta, GA 30066
770-591-2677

Appendix A
Magazines
& Trade Publications

This appendix lists only specialized trade magazines and publications that are not readily available on newsstands. Magazines about computers and the Internet are widely available in many retail locations, therefore such publications are not included here.

Audiotex News
Published monthly by Audiotex News, Inc.,
2362 Hempstead Turnpike, 2nd Floor, East Meadow, NY 11554
Telephone: 516-735-3398
Subscription: Annual: $249 Six-month: $179
This is the leading newsletter for the audiotex industry, published without interruption every month since 1989 in a format which allows it to respond quickly to fast-breaking information and news about the industry. *Audiotex News* is dedicated to circulating independent, unbiased information for and about the pay-per-call industry, setting the standard for clear, concise presentation of information, and analysis of the competitive elements of the 800/900 pay-per-call market.

Computer Telephony
Published monthly by Telecom Library, Inc.,
12 West 21st St., New York, NY 10010
Telephone: 215-355-2886 (subscriptions)
Annual Subscription: $25
Tag-lined "The Magazine for Computer and Telephone Integration," this magazine is targeted at computer professionals—users, software and hardware developers, systems integrators, VARs, network resellers, distributors, consultants, OEM integrators and carriers. Despite its technical focus, this magazine is a good way to keep up with the inexorable trend towards the merging of computer and telecommunications technologies.

InfoText
Published bimonthly by Gordon Publishing, Inc.,
9200 Sunset Blvd., Suite 710, Los Angeles, CA 90069
Telephone: 310-724-6783
Annual Subscription: $64
This magazine is recognized as one of the major trade publications for the pay-per-call and interactive telephone industries. Its tag line reads: "Integrating Electronic Commerce and Communications." *InfoText* contains current topical information relating to all facets of the audiotex industry, including new applications, legal updates, marketing information, and many newsworthy articles.

Outside the Envelope
Published monthly by Hattrick Publishing Group, Inc.,
1220 L Street, N.W., Suite 330, Washington, DC 20005
Telephone: 800-953-1700
Fax-on-Demand Directory: 800-872-1899
Annual Subscription: $24 for print version, free by fax
This newsletter features analysis and comments on developments in the 800, 900, Online, Fax, IVDS and long-distance markets with illustrations and examples of how regulatory policy and carrier actions impact upon information providers. The editor, Warren Miller, is also president of Telecompute Corporation, a

leading service bureau, and has been an active industry leader for many years. The primary emphasis is on pay-per-call, telemarketing, and information delivery applications in the U.S. and Canada. The fax-on-demand system offers numerous brief papers and article reprints on a variety of topical subjects. The materials are offered for free or for only a nominal charge. An excellent source of current information about industry issues.

Teleconnect Magazine
Published monthly by Telecom Library, Inc.,
12 West 21st Street, New York, NY 10010
Telephone: 215-355-2886 (subscriptions); 800-LIBRARY (publications and catalog)
Annual Subscription: $15
This is one of the major trade magazines covering the telecommunications industry, focusing on technology and end-user equipment. According to its tag line, it is "the independent guide to choosing, using and installing telecommunications equipment and services." The Telecom Library also publishes *Call Center* magazine and several telecommunications books that may be of interest to you. Call or write for its catalog.

Phone+
Published monthly by Taurus Publishing, Inc.,
4141 North Scottsdale Road, Suite 316, Scottsdale AZ 85251
Telephone: 602-990-1101
Annual Subscription: $50
This magazine is tag-lined, "The Monthly Journal for the Public Communications Industry," and is targeted at equipment and service providers, with an emphasis on long-distance services and issues.

CommunicationsWeek
InformationWeek
Published weekly by CMP Publications, Inc.,
P.O. Box 1093, Skokie, IL 60076-8093
Telephone: 800-292-3642
Annual subscription:

InformationWeek: $68
CommunicationsWeek: $163

These weekly magazines are written for information and technology managers and businesses—or anyone who needs to stay up-to-date on what is happening on the information superhighway. *InformationWeek* focuses more on content issues, while *CommunicationsWeek* covers the underlying technologies that make it all possible.

Interactive Age
Published biweekly by CMP Publications, Inc.,
(see above)
Annual Subscription: $79

This newspaper covers the entire interactive industry, including the telecommunications, computer, entertainment-media and information industries, and how they are converging. Timely news and information for those who need to stay on top of developments in this fast-changing environment.

Telephony
Published weekly by Intertec Publishing,
P.O. Box 12901, Overland Park, KS 66282-2901
Telephone: 800-441-0294
Annual Subscription: $45

This magazine serves the public telephone network market, and its readers are primarily telecom professionals at the various local, regional and national telephone companies. Although the subject matter is targeted to these people, this is a good magazine for keeping current on what is happening with the carriers. *Telephony* lists *CommunicationsWeek* (see above) as one of its main competitors.

America's Network
Published twice monthly by Advanstar Communications, Inc.,
7500 Old Oak Blvd., Cleveland, OH 44130
Telephone: 800-346-0085 x-477
Annual Subscription: $44

This magazine is targeted at telephone company personnel, covering the issues and technology surrounding the public telephone network. It contains excellent coverage of emerging technologies, particularly the distribution of voice and data over wired and wireless networks, and the challenges faced by the phone companies in bringing them to market. Good reading if you wonder how the phone companies are actually going to deliver all this wonderful multimedia communications to your doorstep.

Telecommunications
Published monthly by Horizon House Publications, Inc.,
685 Canton Street, Norwood, MA 02062
Telephone: 617-769-9750
Annual Subscription: $95
This magazine is tag lined "the technology and business publication for communications professionals." Although it is aimed at information/communications managers at larger companies, it has good coverage of topics of interest to organizations of all sizes, including electronic commerce, public networks, and new technologies.

Intele-Card News
Published bimonthly by Quality Publishing, Inc.,
317 Sawdust Rd., The Woodlands, TX 77380
Telephone: 800-310-7047
Annual Subscription: $39
This is one of two trade magazines covering the prepaid phone card industry. It provides good coverage on what is happening in this market and who the players are.

TeleCard World
Published monthly by MuliMedia Publishing Corp.,
P.O. Box 42190, Houston, TX 77242
Telephone: 713-974-5252
Annual Subscription: $36
This is the second of two trade magazines covering the prepaid phone card industry. This magazine also sponsors a major trade show every year.

Appendix B
Books & Directories

This appendix is not intended to list every resource that exists about the topics covered in this book. It is limited to books that are difficult to find in bookstores and libraries because the subjects are fairly specialized. For example, there are no Internet books listed here because you will find scores of good titles on this subject at any bookstore.

General Reading

Telecommunications Factbook
By Joseph A. Pecar, Roger J. O'Connor, and David A. Garbin
Published by McGraw-Hill, Inc.,
1221 Avenue of the Americas, New York, NY 10020
This is an excellent overall primer on the public telecommunications network and how it works, written in easy-to-understand, non-technical language for beginners as well as professionals.

Newton's Telecom Dictionary
By Harry Newton
Published by the Telecom Library, Inc.,

12 West 21st St., New York, NY 10010
Telephone: 800-LIBRARY
Price: $29.95
This massive 755-page volume was written by Harry Newton, publisher of *Teleconnect, Call Center* and *Imaging* magazines, in an easy-to-read non-technical style. This is an everyday working dictionary for anyone involved in telecommunications. The user-friendly prose reads more like a good tutorial than a technical dictionary, and you'll never be confused again with the arcane language of the telecommunications industry.

Telecom Made Easy:
Money-Saving, Profit-Building Solutions for Home Businesses, Telecommuters and Small Organizations
By June Langhoff
Published by Aegis Publishing Group, Ltd.,
796 Aquidneck Ave., Newport, RI 02842
Telephone: 401-849-4200; 800-828-6961   Fax: 401-849-4231
Price: $19.95
This is an easy-to-understand guide to getting the most out of telephone products and services. It is specifically written for small businesses, offices and organizations with fewer than five phone lines, who don't have telecom managers or the resources that large organizations have, but who still want to sound like them. Covers all the latest telecom products and services that are available, in simple, non-technical language, and how to put them together to best serve your specific needs.

Telecom Business Opportunities
By Steve Rosenbush
Published by Aegis Publishing Group, Ltd.,
796 Aquidneck Ave., Newport, RI 02842-7246
Telephone: 800-828-6961; fax: 401-849-4231
Price: $24.95
This book explains where the money will be made in the exploding $200 billion telecommunications industry. *USA Today* telecom reporter Steve Rosenbush tells us about fascinating entrepreneurs who are carving out their share of profits in this

newly deregulated industry, and where the next fortunes will be made.

Telecom Glossary
By Marc Robins
Published by Aegis Publishing Group,
796 Aquidneck Ave., Newport, RI 02842-7246
Telephone: 800-828-6961; fax: 401-849-4231
Price: $9.95
An easy-to-understand guide to the terminology of the telecom industry. Explains the technology for non-technical business people who need to understand enough to make informed decisions about what technologies to adopt in their businesses.

Megamedia Shakeout
By Kevin Maney
Published by John Wiley & Sons, Inc.,
605 Third Ave., New York, NY 10158-0012
Price: $24.95
Provides a good big picture of the major trends in the overall telecommunications industry. The book is subtitled "The inside story of the leaders and the losers in the exploding communications industry."

Highway of Dreams
By A. Michael Noll
Published by Lawrence Erlbaum Associates, Inc.,
10 Industrial Ave., Mahwah, NJ 07430
Telephone: 201-236-9500
This book provides an excellent overview of the telecommunications industry, where it has been and where it is headed. Takes a realistic look at what the technology is really capable of delivering, and debunks some of the hype surrounding the information superhighway.

Technology and Services

The Voice Response Reference Manual & Buyer's Guide
By Marc Robins
Published by Robins Press,
2675 Henry Hudson Pkwy., West, Ste. 6J, Riverdale, NY 10463
Price: $85
Telephone: 800-238-7130
This reference book is a complete resource for interactive voice technology, vendors and systems. It provides up-to-date information necessary for purchasing or building a voice response system. Included are comprehensive equipment vendor profiles and surveys on more than 50 vendors and 60 systems. Hardware and software specifications, configurations and pricing, host computer interfaces, user management features, and selection and implementation advice are all included. Updated regularly.

PC-Telephony
By Bob Edgar
Published by Flatiron Publishing, Inc.
12 West 21st Street, New York, NY 10010
Telephone: 800-LIBRARY
Price: $34.95
Previous editions of this book were titled *PC-Based Voice Processing*. This is the first book written exclusively about voice processing, aimed at the developer of a PC-based voice processing or computer telephony system.

Phone Company Services
By June Langhoff
Published by Aegis Publishing Group,
796 Aquidneck Ave., Newport, RI 02842-7246
Telephone: 800-828-6961; fax: 401-849-4231
Price: $9.95
This book provides a comprehensive listing of all the various services provided by telephone companies, and how to put them to use.

Audiotex News Resource Guide
Published by Audiotex Publishing, Inc.,
2362 Hempstead Turnpike, 2nd Floor, East Meadow, NY 11554
Telephone: 800-735-3398; 516-735-3398   Fax 516-735-3682
Price: $50
This is the only up-to-date comprehensive reference guide for the entire industry, including pay-per-call, automated voice response, computer telephony and voice information services. Features service bureaus, regulatory agencies, telephone companies, advertising agencies, hardware & software systems and components, publications, industry events and every other source you need.

International Callback Book
By Gene Retske
Published by Flatiron Publishing, Inc.
12 West 21st Street, New York, NY 10010
Telephone: 800-999-0345
Price: $34.95
The only book on the subject, it covers using callback, barriers, selecting equipment, selecting a callback company, and all the issues surrounding this industry segment.

Understanding Computer Telephony
By Carlton Carden
Published by Flatiron Publishing, Inc.
12 West 21st Street, New York, NY 10010
Telephone: 800-999-0345
Price: $34.95
Explains computer telephony technology in simple terms. Written for both new value added resellers (VARs) and industry veterans who need to better understand what the technology is capable of delivering.

Computer Telephony:
Automating Home Offices and Small Business
By Ed Tittel and Dawn Rader
Published by AP Professional

Academic Press, 1250 Sixth Ave., San Diego, CA 92101
Telephone: 800-321-5068
Price: $24.95
This book outlines what the technology is all about, who should use it, and how to set up a system. It teaches users how to install, maintain and troubleshoot the system. Includes a comprehensive vendor, distributor, and consultant resource guide.

Computer Telephony Strategies
By Jeffrey R. Shapiro
Published by IDG Books Wordwide, Inc.
155 Bovet Rd., San Mateo, CA 94402
Telephone: 800-762-2974
Price: $34.95
A guide for integrating computers and the enterprise network with the telephone system. Covers computer telephony components, including PBXs, operator consoles and control panels, automated attendants, voice messaging systems, and fax systems.

337 Killer Voice Processing Applications
By Edwin Margulies
Published by Flatiron Publishing, Inc.
12 West 21st Street, New York, NY 10010
Telephone: 800-999-0345
Price: $34.95
This book is crammed with real-world examples of how companies are using voice processing applications to improve business.

Telecommuting and Workplace Alternatives

The Telecommuter's Advisor
By June Langhoff
Published by Aegis Publishing Group,
796 Aquidneck Ave., Newport, RI 02842-7246
Telephone: 800-828-6961; fax: 401-849-4231
Price: $14.95

This book is written for non-technical telecommuting employees who must learn how to use all the new technology. It makes a good training resource for telecommuting programs.

Making Telecommuting Happen
By Jack M. Nilles
Published by Van Nostrand Reinhold
115 Fifth Ave., New York, NY 10003
This book is helpful for managers and companies that are planning to launch a telecommuting program. Provides guidance on how to properly set up a successful program and monitor employee performance.

The Business Traveler's Survival Guide
By June Langhoff
Published by Aegis Publishing Group,
796 Aquidneck Ave., Newport, RI 02842-7246
Telephone: 800-828-6961; fax: 401-849-4231
Price: $9.95
This book covers working on the road, including data security, what to pack in the road warrior's toolkit, what hotels have the best communications setups, and how to stay connected from anywhere, including international travel.

Pay-Per-Call

900 Know-How
By Robert Mastin
Published by Aegis Publishing Group,
796 Aquidneck Ave., Newport, RI 02842-7246
Telephone: 800-828-6961; fax: 401-849-4231
Price: $19.95
This book is widely recognized as the bible of the industry. It covers how to set up a successful pay-per-call service, from selecting a service bureau to promoting the service using free publicity.

Money-Making 900 Numbers:
How Entrepreneurs Use the Telephone to Sell Information
By Carol Morse Ginsburg and Robert Mastin
Published by Aegis Publishing Group,
796 Aquidneck Ave., Newport, RI 02842-7246
Telephone: 800-828-6961; fax: 401-849-4231
Price: $19.95

This book consists of nearly 400 profiles of 900-number programs in 12 different categories: Customer Service & Helping Consumers; Government & Non-Profit Organizations; Professional Services & Advice; Investment, Finance & Business Information; Sports; Environmental Information; Lifestyle, Travel & Leisure; Education, Careers & Self-Improvement; Entertainment; Product & Business Promotion & Marketing; Fundraising & Charity; and News, Politics & Opinions. This book answers the question: What programs are out there, which have been successful and which have failed? The profiles are from one paragraph to several pages in length. An excellent overview of the industry, demonstrating which elements make a successful 900-number program.

Opportunity is Calling:
How to Start Your Own Successful 900 Number
By Bob Bentz
Published by ATS Publishing (1993),
996 Old Eagle School Rd., Suite 1105, Wayne, PA 19087
Telephone: 610-688-6000
Price: $29.95

Written by Bob Bentz, the director of marketing at Advanced Telecom Services, one of the leading 900 service bureaus, this book is quite valuable for serious IPs. In helping establish some 3,000 pay-per-call programs, Bentz has probably seen every conceivable 900 application or idea, from the totally unworkable pie-in-the-sky scheme to the highly imaginative and well-conceived success story.

Glossary

AUDIOTEXT (also Audiotex). This term broadly describes various telecommunications equipment and services that enable users to send or receive information by interacting with a voice processing system via a telephone connection, using audio input. Voice mail, interactive 800 or 900 programs, and telephone banking transactions are examples of applications that fall under this generic category.

AUTOMATIC NUMBER IDENTIFICATION (ANI). A means of identifying the telephone number of the party originating the telephone call, through the use of analog or digital signals which are transmitted along with the call, and equipment that can decipher those signals.

AUTOMATED ATTENDANT. A device, connected to a PBX, which performs simple voice processing functions limited to answering incoming calls and routing them in accordance with the touch-tone menu selections made by the caller.

AUTOMATIC CALL DISTRIBUTOR (ACD). A specialized phone system used for handling a high volume of incoming calls. An ACD will recognize and answer an incoming call, then refer to its programming for instructions on what to do with that call, and then, based on these instructions, it will send the call to a recording giving the caller further instructions or to a voice response unit

(VRU). It can also route the call to a live operator as soon as that operator has completed his/her previous call, perhaps after the caller has heard the recorded message.

CENTRAL OFFICE. Telephone company facility where subscribers' lines are joined to switching equipment for connecting other subscribers to each other, locally and long distance. For example, when making a long distance call, your call first goes to your CO, where it connects to the long distance carrier's network (unless it had to get routed to another CO where the IXC's network is available), and then the call gets routed to a CO near the party you are calling, and then it finishes the trip over the local network connecting the CO with the other party.

CENTREX. A business telephone service offered by a local telephone company from a local central office. Centrex is basically single line telephone service with enhanced features added, allowing a small business with one phone line to have some of the features provided by expensive telephone systems. Those features can include intercom, call forwarding, call transfer, toll restrict, least cost routing and call hold (on single line phones), to name a few.

COMPUTER TELEPHONY. Also known as *Computer-Telephone Integration*. The convergence of computer and telecommunications technologies. Microchips and computers allow for all kinds of sophisticated automated capabilities to be added to the basic telephone. Fax-on-demand, interactive voice response and video conferencing are all the results of computer telephony.

DIALED NUMBER IDENTIFICATION SERVICE (DNIS). DNIS is available on 800 and 900 lines, and is used to identify the numbers dialed (as opposed to caller's number). This would be important if you were a program sponsor with dozens of different 900 numbers tapping into the same program. DNIS allows you to keep track of which numbers are dialed so you can properly compensate your IPs who are promoting your program, or for keeping track of your advertising response using different 900 numbers with different ads.

DUAL TONE MULTI-FREQUENCY (DTMF). The technical term describing push button or touchtone dialing. When you touch a button on a telephone keypad, it makes a tone, which is actually a combination of two tones, one high frequency and one low frequency. Hence the name Dual Tone Multi-Frequency.

ENHANCED SERVICES. Services provided by the telephone company over its network facilities which may be provided without filing a tariff, usually involving some computer related feature such as formatting data or restructuring the information. Also refers to optional services such as Caller ID, Call Forwarding, Call Waiting and Voice Mail.

EXTRANET. A computer network consisting of more than one organization (see INTRANET), such as an industry group or a supplier and its customers. Access is controlled to maintain the security of the network. Dedicated high-speed lines are usually leased from the phone company to link the sites together.

FAX BROADCASTING. An automated system for broadcasting the same fax message to a large number of recipients.

FAX-ON-DEMAND. An automated, computer-based system that allows a caller to select documents, usually from a menu of selections, to be transmitted back to his or her fax machine.

GROUP ACCESS BRIDGING (GAB). Allows three or more callers to join in on a conference type phone call and to participate in the ongoing conversation. The 900 "party" lines are an example of this application.

INTEGRATED SERVICES DIGITAL NETWORK (ISDN). Takes a normal phone line, consisting of a pair of copper wires, and turns it into three high-speed digital circuits. This is accomplished by placing special encoding and decoding equipment at each end of the line.

INTERACTIVE. An audiotext capability that allows the caller to select options from a menu of programmed choices in order to control the flow of information. As the term implies, the caller truly interacts with the computer, following the program instructions and selecting the information he or she wishes to receive.

INTERACTIVE VOICE RESPONSE (IVR). The telephone keypad substitutes for the computer keyboard, allowing anyone with a touch-tone telephone to interact with a computer. Where a computer has a screen for showing the results, IVR uses a digitized synthesized voice to "read" the screen to the caller.

INTEREXCHANGE CARRIER (IXC). This term technically applies to carriers that provide telephone service between LATAs (see below). Long distance companies such as AT&T, Sprint, and MCI are also known as interexchange carriers.

INTERNATIONAL CALLBACK. Used by businesses and travelers in foreign countries that have high international calling rates. Using a pre-assigned, dedicated phone number, you dial your callback service, located in the States, and hang up after one ring. Because you hang up after only one ring, without actually completing the call, the local phone company cannot charge you for a completed call. However, that one ring is enough to signal the switch/computer that you called, seeking dialtone to set up a call.

Recognizing your pre-assigned call-in number, the switch/computer is programmed to immediately dial you back at the phone number you previously designated, referred to as your *callback number*. You now have dialtone that originates in the U.S. Then you will be prompted by the switch/computer to enter the phone number you want to call. Once this is accomplished, the call is set up, consisting of two legs that both originate in the U.S: one to your location and another to the party you are calling.

INTERNET SERVICE PROVIDER (ISP). An organization that offers access to the Internet, through a dial-up telephone modem connection, to its customers, usually for a fee. Independent businesses, online service providers, such as AOL, and phone companies offer this service.

INTRANET. A computer network limited to one company or organization. It can be limited to one building or spread out across the country, using high-speed leased lines provided by the phone company. Access is carefully controlled, and the network is often protected by a *firewall*, which makes it difficult for hackers to gain access.

LOCAL ACCESS TRANSPORT AREA (LATA). This is a geographic service area that generally conforms to standard metropolitan and statistical areas (SMSAs), and some 200 were created with the breakup of AT&T. The local telephone companies provide service within each LATA (Intra-LATA), while a long distance carrier (IXC) must be used for service between LATAs (Inter-LATA).

LOCAL EXCHANGE CARRIER (LEC). This is the local telephone company that provides service within each LATA. Also included in this category are independent LECs such as General Telephone (GTE). The LEC handles all billing and collections within its LATA, often including long distance charges (Inter-LATA), which are collected and forwarded to the appropriate interexchange carriers.

MODEM. A device that translates digital messages from your computer into analog messages that can be sent over regular analog (POTS) phone lines. Another modem at the other end of the line will re-convert the message back into digital form so that the receiving computer can decipher the message.

NORTH AMERICAN NUMBERING PLAN. The method of identifying telephone trunks and assigning service access codes (area codes) in the public network of North America, also known as World Numbering Zone 1.

ONLINE CALL DETAIL DATA (OCDD). Information summarizing inbound calling data, typically detailing call volumes originating from different telephone area codes or states. Useful for tracking response rates to regional advertising.

PAY-PER-CALL. The caller pays a pre-determined charge for accessing information services. 900 is not the only type of pay-per-call service available. For local, intra-LATA applications, a seven digit number is available with a 976 or 540 prefix. This service is usually quite a bit less expensive than long distance 900 services, and should be seriously considered for any local or regional pay-per-call applications that will not have the potential for expanding nationwide.

Pay-per-call services may also be offered over 800 or regular toll lines using credit card or other third party billing mechanisms. When the caller pays a premium above the regular transport charges for the information content of the program, regardless of how payment is made, it is considered a pay-per-call service.

PERSONAL COMMUNICATIONS SERVICES (PCS). A new digital wireless cellular service over a new frequency spectrum recently auctioned off by the FCC. Offers superior digital communications for both voice and data.

PERSONAL DIGITAL ASSISTANT (PDA). Multi-function communications device that looks like a little palmtop computer, which may perform calendar, memo pad, calculator, and scheduling functions, as well as e-mail and paging.

PREPAID DEBIT CARD. See PREPAID PHONE CARD.

PREPAID PHONE CARD. A card with a pre-determined number of minutes or message units, normally used for long-distance calling. The card is tied to a prepaid phone card *platform*, which is essentially a computer that accepts the inbound call from the cardholder (usually via a toll-free 800 number), routes the outbound call to the desired party, keeps track of the message units consumed and remaining, and alerts the caller at certain intervals as the message units are depleted. Some prepaid phone cards also have a replenishment feature, where the cardholder can call into the system and buy additional message units with a credit card, using an IVR system to input all the data and to complete the transaction.

PORT. For the purpose of this book, the interface between a voice processing system and a communications or transmission facility. For all practical purposes, the same thing as a telephone line.

POTS. Plain Old Telephone Service. The basic service supplying standard single line telephones, telephone lines and access to the public switched network. No enhanced services.

PRIVATE BRANCH EXCHANGE (PBX). PBX is a private telephone switching system (as opposed to public), usually located in an organization's premises, with an attendant console. It is connected to a group of lines from one or more central offices to provide services to a number of individual phones, such as in a hotel, business or government office.

REGIONAL BELL OPERATING COMPANY (RBOC). These are the seven holding companies that were created by the breakup of AT&T (also known as Baby Bells):
1. NYNEX
2. Bell Atlantic
3. AMERITECH
4. Bell South
5. Southwestern Bell Corp.
6. U.S. West
7. Pacific Telesis

These companies own many of the various LECs. For example, NYNEX owns both New England Telephone and New York Telephone. However, there are numerous independent LECs that are not owned by any RBOC. For example, Southern New England Telecommunications Corp. (SNET) is an independent LEC serving most of Connecticut's residential customers, and has nothing to do with NYNEX.

SERVICE BUREAU. A company that provides voice processing / call handling / audiotext equipment and services and connection to telephone network facilities. These companies can offer a variety of communications services, such as fax-on-demand, fax broadcasting, international callback, prepaid phone cards, IVR programs, 900 services, automated order processing and other related services. An alternative to purchasing equipment and operating such services in-house.

T-1 Also spelled T1. A digital transmission link with a capacity of 1.544 Mbps (1,544,000 bits per second). T-1 normally can handle 24 simultaneous voice conversations over two pairs of wires, like the ones serving your house, each one digitized at 64 Kbps. This is accomplished by using special encoding and decoding equipment at each end of the transmission path. T-1 is a standard for digital transmission in North America.

TARIFF. Documents filed by a regulated telephone company with a state public utility commission or the Federal Communications Commission. The tariff, a public document, describes and details services, equipment and pricing offered by the telephone company (a common carrier) to all potential customers. As a "common carrier," the telephone company must offer its services to the general public at the prices and conditions outlined in its tariffs.

TELECARD. See PREPAID PHONE CARD.

TRUNK. A communication line between two switching systems. The term switching systems typically includes equipment in a central office (the telephone company) and PBXs. A tie trunk connects PBXs, while central office trunks connect a PBX to the switching system at the central office.

VARI-A-BILL. A 900 service of AT&T whereby the call price varies depending on the caller's selection of menu choices. This allows the IP to charge more fairly for information of varying value, such as live technical advice versus recorded instructions.

VIDEO CONFERENCING. The PC-based desktop models of this equipment consist of a little video camera mounted on the monitor, a video card, speakers and software to make it all work. The software may also support *document conferencing*, where both parties can work on the same document simultaneously, each seeing what the other changes on the document. This technology works best on higher-speed connections such as ISDN, because the performance on regular analog phone lines is fuzzy, jerky and slow.

VOICE MAIL SYSTEM. A computerized system that records, stores and retrieves voice messages. You can program the system (voice mail boxes) to forward messages, leave messages for inbound callers, add comments and deliver messages to you, etc. It is essentially a sophisticated answering machine for a large business with multiple phone lines (probably with a PBX), or it can be a network-based service provided by the phone company.

VOICE PROCESSING. This is the general term encompassing the use of the telephone to communicate with a computer by way of the touch-tone keypad and synthesized voice response. Audiotex, speech recognition and IVR are subclassifications under voice processing.

VOICE RECOGNITION. Also known as *Speech Recognition*, the ability of a computer to recognize human speech and the spoken word.

VOICE RESPONSE UNIT (VRU). This is the building block of any voice processing system, essentially a voice computer. Instead of a computer keyboard for entering information (commands), a VRU uses remote touchtone telephones. Instead of a screen for showing the results, a VRU uses synthesized voice to "read" the information to the caller.

Other Books From Aegis Publishing Group:

Aegis Publishing specializes in telecommunications books for non-technical end-users such as entrepreneurs, small businesses, telecommuters and the SOHO (Small Office/Home Office) market. Inquire about wholesale quantity discounts:

Aegis Publishing Group, Ltd.
796 Aquidneck Avenue, Newport, RI 02842
800-828-6961; aegis@aegisbooks.com
Web site: www.aegisbooks.com

Telecom Business Opportunities:
The Entrepreneur's Guide to Making Money in the Telecommunications Revolution (December 1997), by Steven Rosenbush
Item TC10 $24.95
ISBN: 1-890154-04-0, paper, 336 pages, 5-1/2" x 8-1/2"
This first-of-its-kind guide by *USA Today* telecom reporter Steve Rosenbush shows where the money is to be made in the evolving, deregulated telecommunications industry. Consists of fascinating case studies of real-life entrepreneurs who are carving out their share of profits in this enormous $123 billion industry. Covers the implications of—and the opportunities created by—the Telecommunications Reform Act of 1996. From long-distance resellers to competitive access providers, from PCS services to TeleCards, from service bureaus to Internet service providers, this book shows where the hottest opportunities are to be found in this burgeoning industry.

Telecom Made Easy:
Money-Saving, Profit-Building Solutions
for Home Businesses, Telecommuters and Small Organizations
3rd edition (August 1997), by June Langhoff
Item TC19 $19.95
ISBN: 0-9632790-7-6, paper, 400 pages, 5-1/2" x 8-1/2"
Find out how to benefit from the latest technology, from basic wiring options and answering devices to ISDN and going online. "... a basic but thorough guide to phone systems and services, cellular phones, answering devices, paging, on-line services, modems, faxes, and networked systems... geared toward home businesses, telecommuters, and small firms." —*Nation's Business*

The Telecommuter's Advisor:
Working in the Fast Lane (July 1996), by June Langhoff
Item TC2 $14.95
ISBN: 0-9632790-5-X, paper, 240 pages, 5-1/2" x 8-1/2"
". . . practical, 1990s real-world advice. . . This book is for anyone who wants to improve their remote working skills and covers a broad range of topics, including designing a home office, selecting equipment, coping with e-mail, using groupware and wireless communications, and connecting internationally. . ." —*Booklist*

Phone Company Services:
Working Smarter with the Right Telecom Tools
(September 1997), by June Langhoff
Item TC7 $9.95
ISBN: 1-890154-01-6, paper, 96 pages, 5-1/2" x 8-1/2"
From Call Forwarding to Caller ID to 500 Service to ISDN to Centrex, this book describes phone company services in detail, and how to put them to their best use in real-life applications.

900 KNOW-HOW:
How to Succeed With Your Own 900 Number Business
3rd edition (August 1996), by Robert Mastin
Item TC1B $19.95
ISBN: 0-9632790-3-3, paper, 350 pages, 5-1/2" x 8-1/2"
Become a toll collector on the info highway. "If you have decided that you are nothing but road kill on the information highway, take a look at *900 Know-How* . . . For those in the information-providing business, the 900 number could be an attractive source of revenue." —*Wall Street Journal*

Getting the Most From Your Yellow Pages Advertising:
Maximum Profits at Minimum Cost
2nd edition (December 1997), by Barry Maher
Item TC14 $19.95
ISBN: 1-890154-05-9, paper, 304 pages, 5-1/2" x 8-1/2"
Completely updated second edition to the perennial bible on the subject. "Barry Maher has helped thousands of small businesses get the most effective and cost-effective Yellow Pages advertising possible. Easily the most widely respected consultant, speaker and writer on the subject. . ." —*Time*. "The definitive book on the subject." —*Home Office Computing*

Telecom Glossary:
Understanding Telecommunications Technology
(September 1997), by Marc Robins
Item TC8 $9.95
ISBN: 1-890154-02-4, paper, 96 pages, 5-1/2" x 8-1/2"
Ever wonder what *Asynchronous Transfer Mode* really means? Or how *ISDN* can help your business? Or what *Computer Telephony Integration* is all about? This glossary of telecom terms will de-mystify the arcane language of telecommunications so that non-technical end users will understand what it all means and how to put it to use in solving every-day business challenges.

The Business Traveler's Survival Guide:
How to Get Work Done While on the Road
(October 1997), by June Langhoff
Item TC9 $9.95
ISBN: 1-890154-03-2, paper, 112 pages, 5-1/2" x 8-1/2"
This handy guide will be appreciated by every business traveller, covering remote working, data security, what to pack in the road warrior's toolkit, and a listing of business hotels with the best communications setups. The ideal travel companion.

Money-Making 900 Numbers:
How Entrepreneurs Use the Telephone to Sell Information
(July 1995), by Carol Morse Ginsburg and Robert Mastin
Item TC18 $19.95
ISBN: 0-9632790-1-7, paper, 336 pages, 5-1/2" x 8-1/2"
"... a thorough job of illustrating the incredible variety of pay-per-call services that have been done... an excellent overall view of the industry, and anyone thinking of starting a 900 number should read the book."
—*McHenry County Business Journal*